The Rise of Brandenburg–Prussia

IN THE SAME SERIES

General Editors: Eric J. Evans and P.D. King

For Chris

The Rise of
Brandenburg–Prussia

Margaret Shennan

London and New York

First published 1995
by Routledge
11 New Fetter Lane, London EC4P 4EE

Simultaneously published in the USA and Canada
by Routledge
29 West 35th Street, New York, NY 10001

Typeset in Bembo by
Ponting–Green Publishing Services, Chesham, Bucks
Printed and bound in Great Britain by
Clays Ltd, St Ives PLC

British Library Cataloguing in Publication Data

A catalogue record for this book is available from the British Library

Library of Congress Cataloguing in Publication Data

A catalogue record for this book has been requested

ISBN 0–415–129389

Contents

Foreword

Lancaster Pamphlets offer concise and up-to-date accounts of major historical topics, primarily for the help of students preparing for Advanced Level examinations, though they should also be of value to those pursuing introductory courses in universities and other institutions of higher education. Without being all-embracing, their aims are to bring some of the central themes or problems confronting students and teachers into sharper focus than the textbook writer can hope to do; to provide the reader with some of the results of recent research which the textbook may not embody; and to stimulate thought about the whole interpretation of the topic under discussion.

Time chart

1356   The Golden Bull of Emperor Charles IV confirms the ruler of Brandenburg as one of the seven imperial Electors

1415   Frederick of Hohenzollern appointed Elector of Brandenburg by Emperor Sigismund: the foundation of the Hohenzollern dynasty in Brandenburg

1525   Albert of Hohenzollern, Grand Master of the Order of Teutonic Knights, converted from Catholicism to Lutheranism

1540   As Lutheranism spreads rapidly in Brandenburg, Joachim II (1535–71) declares himself supreme head of the state church

1555   Peace of Augsburg gives tacit recognition to Lutheranism and validates the principle of *cuius regio eius religio*, giving rulers the right to decide the state religion

1571   Accession of Elector John George (–1598), a fervent Lutheran

1591   Marriage of electoral heir, John Sigismund, to Anne of Prussia, eldest daughter of Duke Albert Frederick

1603   Pact of Gera: Hohenzollern family confirms principles of primogeniture and indivisibility of dynastic territories

1604   Elector Joachim Frederick (1598–1608) establishes the Privy Council (*Geheimer Rat*) to circumvent power of the nobility

1609	Duke of Cleves–Jülich dies, leading to succession dispute between Elector of Brandenburg and Duke of Pfalz–Neuburg
1611	Sigismund III of Poland invests Elector John Sigismund (1608–19) as heir to the ducal fief of East Prussia
1613	Elector John Sigismund becomes a Calvinist
1614	Treaty of Xanten: compromise partition of Cleves–Jülich gives Cleves, Mark and Ravensburg to Brandenburg
1618	On death of Duke Albert Frederick of Prussia, Elector John Sigismund succeeds to the duchy of East Prussia; Bohemian nobles reject the Habsburg claim to the Bohemian throne, thereby effectively provoking the Thirty Years War
1619	Death of Elector John Sigismund; George William (1619–40) becomes Elector of Brandenburg and Duke of Prussia; Frederick V, the Calvinist Elector Palatine elected King of Bohemia; Habsburg Ferdinand II elected Emperor
1621	Spanish forces devastate Cleves and Mark; Dutch troops invade to defend the principalities from Spain
1625–6	George William remains neutral in the Danish War
1626	George William confirms loyalty to Emperor Ferdinand II; Swedish troops invade Brandenburg
1626–7	Brandenburg ravaged by Wallenstein's army
1629	Edict of Restitution asserts imperial authority over Empire and threatens Protestant lands secularized since 1552
1630	Gustavus Adolphus of Sweden enters the war in Germany; George William's minister, Schwartzenberg, drops the Privy Council in favour of a new War Council (*Kriegsrat*)
1631	Storming of Frankfurt-on-Oder and sacking of Magdeburg; Swedish troops invest Berlin; George William forced to abandon neutrality and join Swedish alliance
1632	Death of Gustavus Adolphus of Sweden at the battle of Lützen
1633	League of Heilbronn: Protestant German states forced to join Sweden; George William resists membership despite Swedish plan for marriage of Frederick William of Brandenburg and Christina of Sweden

1635	Peace of Prague between Emperor Ferdinand and German princes modifies Treaty of Restitution (1627 replaces 1552 as criterion for possession of ecclesiastical lands); George William rejoins the imperial alliance
1636–7	Swedish armies again occupy Brandenburg
1637	Duke of Pomerania dies; Swedish occupation of Pomerania prevents George William's succession; the Elector takes refuge in Prussia; Cleves Estates repudiate Dutch alliance
1640	Death of Elector George William and accession of his son, Frederick William I (1640–88); the Privy Council restored
1640–41	Diet of Regensburg
1641	Frederick William repudiates Peace of Prague and imperial alliance; death of Schwartzenberg
1644	Armistice between Brandenburg and Sweden; general peace negotiations begin at Münster and Osnabrück (Westphalia)
1645	Frederick William mediates Peace of Brömsebro between Sweden and Denmark
1646	Brandenburg troops invade duchy of Berg but forced to withdraw because of hostility of Cleves Estates
1648	Peace of Westphalia: Brandenburg receives East Pomerania, secularized bishoprics of Halberstadt, Minden, Kammin and the reversion of the city of Magdeburg on the death of its coadjutor-archbishop
1649	Frederick William makes concessions in Recess of 1649 to Cleves Estates
1650	Treaty of Nürnburg finalizes land details of Westphalia
1651	Frederick William again attacks Jülich–Berg but thwarted by Cleves Estates; Emperor Ferdinand III ·mediates
1653	Recess of Brandenburg: electoral compromise with Brandenburg Estates; Treaty of Stettin settles partition of Pomerania
1655	Frederick William concludes defensive alliance with Dutch; start of first Nordic War; origin of the new General War Office (*Generalkriegskommissariat*) under Claus von Platen

1656	Treaty of Königsberg: Ducal Prussia becomes a Swedish fief; Treaty of Marienburg: Brandenburg gives military aid to Sweden against Poland at the battle of Warsaw; Treaty of Labiau: Charles X of Sweden recognizes Frederick William as sovereign Duke of Prussia
1657	Treaty of Wehlau: King of Poland recognizes Frederick William as sovereign Duke of Prussia
1658	Frederick William joins anti-Swedish campaign in Denmark and Pomerania; Leopold I (–1705) elected Emperor; German princes form League of the Rhine
1660	Peace of Oliva: in return for giving up Pomeranian conquests Frederick William gains universal recognition of sovereignty in ducal Prussia; Regency in Sweden after death of Charles X
1660–61	Recess of 1660–61: compromise with Cleves Estates
1661	Leader of Königsberg burghers, Hieronymous Roth, arrested; clashes between Prussian Estates and Frederick William in Diet 1661–3
1666	Brandenburg settles Cleves–Jülich dispute with Neuburg
1667	Treaty of Berlin between Frederick William and Louis XIV; French overrun Spanish Netherlands: Devolution War (1667–8)
1668	Triple Alliance (Sweden, England and Dutch) against France; Emperor Leopold signs secret partition treaty with Louis XIV
1672	Brandenburg makes anti-French treaty with Dutch; start of Franco–Dutch War (1672–8); French army invades Cleves; Prussian nobles opposed to Frederick William's tax policy; their leader Christian von Kalckstein was executed
1674	Establishment of a Central War Treasury (*Generalkriegskasse*)
1675	Battle of Fehrbellin: Frederick William known from this time as 'the Great Elector'; Brandenburg troops begin the conquest of West Pomerania (–1678).
1677	Brandenburg army captures Stettin from Sweden
1678	Berlin suburb of Dorotheenstadt built
1679	Peace of Saint-Germain-en-Laye between Brandenburg and France: Frederick William has to return all

Pomeranian conquests to Sweden in return for minor gains; concludes a secret alliance with Louis XIV

1680   Madgeburg finally reverts to Brandenburg

1682   African Company established to trade with Guinea coast

1685   Louis XIV repeals Edict of Nantes; Frederick William issues Potsdam Decree offering asylum to French Huguenots; renews Dutch alliance with William of Orange

1686   Frederick William joins in defensive alliance, the League of Augsburg, with Emperor Leopold; makes defensive pact with Charles XI of Sweden

1687   Edict passed to protect manufacture of woollen cloth and prohibit foreign imports of cloth

1688   Death of the Great Elector; Elector Frederick III succeeds; orders the building of the suburb of Friedrichstadt; French occupy Palatinate and declare war on the Dutch; William of Orange invades England; start of the Nine Years War; Frederick urges German princes to form 'Magdeburg Concert' to support Emperor against Louis XIV

1689   Grand Alliance formed; Emperor declares war on France, supported by Brandenburg, Dutch, England (and later Spain and Savoy); Controller's Office (*Geheime Hofkammer*) set up

1693   Recruiting Edict to make provinces responsible for levels of military recruitment

1694   New University of Halle founded; Andreas Schlüter becomes court sculptor

1696   State Academy of Arts established in Berlin

1697   Downfall of Danckelmann and Knyphausen and rise of von Wartenberg as royal favourite; Frederick invites Leibniz to Berlin; Frederick's rival, Augustus of Saxony, elected King of Poland; youthful Charles XII succeeds in Sweden; Treaty of Ryswick concludes Nine Years War

1700   Emperor Leopold recognizes Frederick's claim as King in Prussia; Brandenburg renews 1686 alliance with Empire; Society of Sciences founded in Berlin, with Leibniz as first Director; new Arsenal built in Berlin; death of Charles II of Spain precipitates Spanish Succession crisis; start of the Great Northern War

1720	Treaty of Stockholm: Sweden concedes Western Pomerania, including Stettin, Usedom and Wollin to Prussia
1721	Peace of Nystad concludes Great Northern War; African Company sold to the Dutch
1722	Nobles' sons are encouraged to enter cadet school and register for military service in Table of Vassals
1723	Frederick William sets up a centralized administrative service, the General Directory, merging former institutions, the General War Commissariat and Finance Directory; Christian Wolff expelled from Brandenburg for subversion
1725	Frederick William joins Hanover alliance of France and Great Britain in the Herrenhausen Convention
1726	Treaty of Westerhausen reconciles Brandenburg to Austria and Russia
1728	Treaty of Berlin confirmed Austro-Prussian alliance; in return for Prussia's guarantee of the Pragmatic Sanction, Emperor Charles VI gives moral supporet to Hohenzollern claim to Jülich–Berg
1729	Chairs of Economics founded at universities of Frankfurt-on-Oder and Halle
1731	George II of Great Britain signs treaty of mutual guarantee with Emperor Charles VI
1733	Recruitment Edict introduces cantonal system for military recruitment; War of the Polish Succession (–1735) starts; Frederick William offers military support to Emperor on behalf of Austrian candidate, Augustus II of Saxony
1736	Austro-Turkish War (–1739) breaks out; Frederick William offers financial but no military support to Emperor
1738	C.P.E. Bach appointed court harpsichordist to Crown Prince Frederick
1739	Secret treaty between Frederick William and Cardinal Fleury: France guarantees part of Jülich–Berg inheritance to Prussia
1740	Death of King Frederick William I; accession of Frederick II

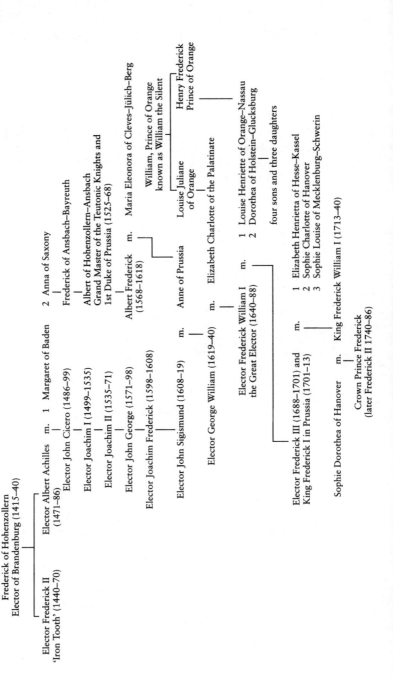

Genealogy of the House of Hohenzollern in Brandenburg–Prussia to 1740

Frederick of Hohenzollern
Elector of Brandenburg (1415–40)

Elector Frederick II
'Iron Tooth' (1440–70)

Elector Albert Achilles   m.   1 Margaret of Baden   2 Anna of Saxony
(1471–86)

Elector John Cicero (1486–99)   Frederick of Ansbach–Bayreuth

Elector Joachim I (1499–1535)   Albert of Hohenzollern–Ansbach
Grand Master of the Teutonic Knights and
Elector Joachim II (1535–71)   1st Duke of Prussia (1525–68)

Elector John George (1571–98)   Albert Frederick   m.   Maria Eleonora of Cleves–Jülich–Berg
(1568–1618)
Elector Joachim Frederick (1598–1608)   William, Prince of Orange
known as William the Silent

Elector John Sigismund (1608–19)   m.   Anne of Prussia   Louise Juliane   Henry Frederick
of Orange   Prince of Orange

Elector George William (1619–40)   m.   Elizabeth Charlotte of the Palatinate

Elector Frederick William I   m.   1 Louise Henriette of Orange–Nassau
the Great Elector (1640–88)   2 Dorothea of Holstein–Glucksburg

four sons and three daughters

Elector Frederick III (1688–1701) and   m.   1 Elizabeth Henrietta of Hesse–Kassel
King Frederick I in Prussia (1701–13)   2 Sophie Charlotte of Hanover
3 Sophie Louise of Mecklenburg–Schwerin

Sophie Dorothea of Hanover   m.   King Frederick William I (1713–40)

Crown Prince Frederick
(later Frederick II 1740–86)

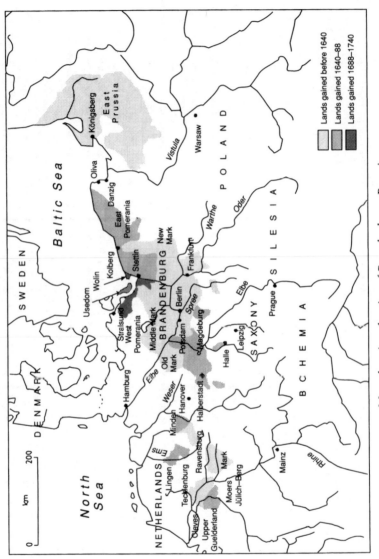

Map showing the rise of Brandenburg–Prussia

Lands gained before 1640
Lands gained 1640–88
Lands gained 1688–1740

North Sea

Baltic Sea

SWEDEN

DENMARK

NETHERLANDS

POLAND

SILESIA

BOHEMIA

SAXONY

BRANDENBURG

East Prussia

Königsberg

Oliva
Danzig

East Pomerania

Kolberg
Wolin
Usedom
Stettin
Stralsund
West Pomerania
Middle Mark
New Mark
Frankfurt
Berlin
Spree
Potsdam
Magdeburg
Halle
Leipzig
Old Mark
Halberstadt
Hamburg
Hanover
Minden
Weser
Ems
Lingen
Ravensberg
Tecklenburg
Mark
Moers
Jülich-Berg
Upper Guelderland
Cleves

Mainz

Prague

Warsaw

Vistula

Oder

Warthe

Elbe

Rhine

km
0   200

Introduction

The general historical context

The contribution of Prussia to the German Reich in modern European history has spurred historians to look back with a questioning eye at the dynamic development of its predecessor, Brandenburg–Prussia, during the early modern period. The transformation of an insignificant north German state to the status of a major European power is an epic theme and one which appears to follow a certain logical progression. There has been a tendency to attribute its evolution to a fortuitous sequence of astute, able-bodied rulers, from the Elector Frederick William I (1640–88) to King Frederick II (1740–86), who understood and exploited the realities of power-politics. The success of these Hohenzollern princes lay in their creation of a strong military machine, supported by rigorous taxation, an efficient bureaucracy and a co-operative nobility, the junker class. By the end of the eighteenth century it could be said that Brandenburg–Prussia had established a particular tradition of successful militarism and autocracy. It had also achieved political parity with Austria within the Holy Roman Empire. The Hohenzollerns had thrown down the gauntlet to the Imperial Habsburgs for dominance in Germany.

However, three-quarters of a century were to pass before the duality of Prussia and Austria was resolved. Their rivalry was

1

interrupted by the French Revolution and the Napoleonic Wars, which brought the collapse of the old order in Germany. The first Reich, the Holy Roman Empire, was swept away in 1806; neither Prussia nor Austria could resist the military might of France under Napoleon Bonaparte. Yet after 1815 both powers were involved in the reconstruction of Germany and in the constitution of a Confederation of thirty-nine states. Meanwhile, in an apparently prophetic manifesto of 1812, Stein, chief minister to King Frederick William III, indicated a modern role for Prussia, which would harness German national consciousness. He declared his wish 'that Germany shall be great and strong. . . . My creed is unity' (8, p. 406). Even so, unity took some decades to achieve. Success came finally through Bismarck's consistent pursuit of Prussian interests, or, in his own notorious phrase, through 'blood and iron'. In 1871 King William I was proclaimed Emperor, or Kaiser, of the second German Empire; Austro–Hungary was excluded.

The new German Empire was, according to one expert, 'a Prussian Reich, shaped to accord with Prussian interests, constructed in conformity with Prussian traditions, ruled by the dynasty of Hohenzollern and dominated by the Prussian Junker class' (8, pp. 422–3). It is not surprising, therefore, that historians like Johann Gustav Droysen and Heinrich von Treitschke regarded German unification under Prussian hegemony as the natural working out of the historical process. Just as English Whig historians tended to interpret Britain's development as one of progressive evolution towards constitutional democracy, the exponents of the so-called Borussian legend equated progress with political unity and depicted the natural destiny of Hohenzollern Prussia as to lead and unite the German people (11, p. xi).

Today, such a view of German history is decidedly outmoded. It was being questioned by some even before the final defeat and collapse in 1918 of the second German empire; and the failure of first the Weimar Republic in 1933 and then Hitler's Third Reich in 1945 brought many more to reconsider their assumptions, in the search for a new political model for Germany. Consequently, since 1945 a new generation of historians has been re-assessing Germany's past. Recent events in Europe – the thawing of the Cold War, the ending of the postwar division of Germany into the German Democratic Republic and the Federal

Republic of Germany, and the ensuing peaceful reunification of Germany – are bound to refuel the debate. The shape of Germany's present and future inevitably reopens questions about Germany's past. The part played by the Prussian state in that past cannot be swept aside as irrelevant. But the context for studying the rise of Brandenburg–Prussia in the seventeenth and eighteenth centuries should be free of nineteenth-century predeterminism.

The division of history into 'reigns' is an artificial device, and while it is sometimes convenient to resort to it, certain provisos should be made. The study of a particular ruler sheds light on a relatively narrow spectrum of human activity. In the case of the Hohenzollerns, electors and kings may have formulated policies and been actively involved in carrying them out, but that is only a part of the story. The social and economic structure of society with which they had to contend, the diversity of internal pressures and the intricacies of external relations, the geographical accidents of terrain, boundaries and climate, prevailing ethical and cultural influences, and, last but not least, the curious impact of perversity and chance: all these are factors contributing to the emergence of the state of Brandenburg–Prussia.

1618: a starting point?

The term 'Brandenburg–Prussia' relates to the history of the seventeenth and eighteenth centuries, but it is the intention of this study to focus on the process of state-building during the period 1618–1740. Taking three considerations into account, the year 1618 is a persuasive starting point. In the first place, it marked an important stage in the dynastic consolidation of the Hohenzollern lands, the historic union of Brandenburg and Prussia, which laid the foundation of a single state. In addition, the decades prior to 1618 were a natural prologue to the reign of Elector George William (1619–40) and his successors: many of the issues which would influence Hohenzollern policy well into the eighteenth century, were in evidence at his accession. And finally, 1618 was the year which highlighted the growing polarization of Europe and plunged Germany, including Brandenburg–Prussia, involuntarily into the Thirty Years War.

The land-locked state or Mark of Brandenburg straddled the north European plain and the rivers Elbe and Oder. In the mid-fourteenth century, its status was enhanced when its ruler, the margrave, was confirmed as one of seven imperial electors. The year 1415 was another landmark: the Emperor appointed one of his loyal henchmen, Frederick of Hohenzollern, to rule Brandenburg, conferring the title of Elector upon him. In one stroke, a new, dynamic dynasty was established, that was to survive until 1918. Frederick's successor, Albert Achilles (1471–86), a ruthless and ambitious dynast, set a precedent for the Hohenzollerns. He strengthened the prince's authority by establishing that the main function of the *Landtag*, the assembly of the Estates, was to vote taxes for the administration and defence of the realm. He also instituted a law of primogeniture to safeguard the succession (1473) and enforced his suzerainty over neighbouring Pomerania.

The province of East Prussia was by then a fief of the Polish crown and lay outside the German Empire. Abutting the Baltic Sea, it was ruled by a religious order of crusaders, the Teutonic Knights, and was separated from Brandenburg by the lands of Poland and Pomerania. At the Reformation the order was secularized, and in 1525 the Grand Master, Albert of Hohenzollern, a convert to Lutheranism, became the first Duke of Prussia and married to perpetuate his line. It was the marriage of his eldest granddaughter, Anne of Prussia, to John Sigismund of Brandenburg in 1591, that brought about the union of the two Hohenzollern principalities. The succession of the Brandenburg line was virtually assured after an agreement of 1578, and it was confirmed in 1611 when the King of Poland recognized John Sigismund as heir to Anne's deranged father, Duke Albert Frederick. Accordingly, when the duke died in 1618, John Sigismund succeeded to the duchy. It was the culmination of a decade of successful aggrandisement.

Anne of Prussia was a crucial figure in dynastic politics. As the niece of the childless Duke of Cleves–Jülich, she was also heiress to two rich and strategic duchies in the region of the lower Rhine. In 1609, on the death of the duke, John Sigismund of Brandenburg expected to take possession of her inheritance. Although his claim was challenged by a rival, the Duke of Pfalz–Neuburg, a compromise was eventually reached. In 1614 the elector took control of the city and duchy of Cleves, together with the adjacent counties of Mark and Ravensburg, and reluctantly conceded the other territories, Jülich–Berg, to the Neuburg claimant. His successors would revive claims to the whole inheritance, but by occupying Cleves, Mark and Ravensburg, Brandenburg gained a significant foothold in the west, and before he died in 1619, John Sigismund could boast of possessions that stretched from the river Rhine to the river Niemen on Europe's Baltic flank.

Dynasticism was one important element in Brandenburg's expansion, but the sixteenth-century Reformation had complicated the political balance of power in both Brandenburg and Prussia. Even in an age of spirituality, religious motives mingled with socio-economic and political considerations. To some degree the rulers successfully exploited religious change. Under Duke Albert of Hohenzollern, Konigsberg became a seat of Protestant learning. Joachim II (1535–71) set up a state church, and, as its supreme head, exercised greater authority over the clergy than any previous ruler. Like Henry VIII of England, he aimed to take over lucrative possessions of the Catholic Church, the archbishopric of Magdeburg and bishopric of Halberstadt being his chief targets. Despite making slow progress, Elector Joachim's efforts ensured that his successors persisted for another century until they acquired these two strategic sees.

Yet the Reformation also brought about political and economic developments which the princes found difficult to control. Encouraged by rising grain prices, the nobility saw the secularization of church property and lands as a legitimate means of consolidating their estates, boosting their wealth and extending their rights over an enserfed peasantry. In both Prussia and Brandenburg the rulers clashed repeatedly with the Estates, the representatives of the noble and burgher classes. To strengthen the dynasty, in 1603 Elector Joachim Frederick II (1598–1608) reaffirmed the principles of primogeniture and the indivisibility of the Hohenzollern possessions in a family agreement, the Pact of Gera. The following year he tried to circumvent the political influence of the great nobles by setting up an inner ring of personal advisers, the Privy Council or *Geheimer Rat*, to counter the power of the Estates. However, under his successor a religious issue reopened the question of the ruler's authority. In 1613 John Sigismund (1608–19) gave up Lutheranism – the religion of the majority in Brandenburg – in favour of Calvinism, an austere and uncompromising form of Protestantism. Although the Elector agreed not to impose the Calvinist faith on his subjects, the high nobility were determined to safeguard their interests and seized control of the Privy Council. John Sigismund's last years were clouded by palace intrigue and by physical and mental disability. As a result, he bequeathed a domestic legacy of diminished authority. The tensions between the ruler and the Estates would continue to be a political problem for another fifty years or more.

Meanwhile, the internal problem of authority was paralleled by religious division in Germany that had intensified since the Peace of Augsburg (1555). With the rise of Calvinism and the revival of Catholicism through the Counter Reformation, rulers took sides in two rival camps, a Protestant Union and a Catholic League. The polarity was underlined when John Sigismund turned to Calvinism, which won him support in the Dutch Republic, while his rival, the duke of Neuburg, was converted to Catholicism to win the backing of the Catholic League. So the Cleves–Jülich crisis, which began in 1609 as a dynastic quarrel, threatened to become a religious and political conflict, since the lower Rhine was a region where Catholic and Protestant subjects, and Spanish, Dutch, French and German political interests, all converged. John Sigismund was doubly vulnerable. Spanish troops occupied key fortresses in Cleves, forcing him in 1616 to call in his Dutch allies and pawn lands and revenues in return for their help, a sensitive situation to be repeated in the future. It was clear after 1618 that the rulers of Brandenburg–Prussia could not confine themselves to German and imperial matters, but would be drawn inexorably into the politics of the lower Rhine and the Baltic, where there were outstanding power issues to be settled. In 1618 these were aggravated by a crisis in central Europe, when the Bohemian nobility defiantly rejected the Habsburg claim to the Bohemian throne. John Sigismund was reluctant to support them against the Emperor and risk undermining the peace of the Empire. One of his last political acts, in 1619, was to support Ferdinand II's election as Emperor, but by this time the Thirty Years War was already under way.

1

THE THIRTY YEARS WAR 1618–48

Internal problems and strategies 1618–40

When Elector George William (1619–40) succeeded John Sigismund in 1619 he was just as wary as his father of becoming
embroiled in the Bohemian crisis. Earlier that year the Bohemian
Estates had elected Frederick V of the Palatinate as their king,
in defiance of the Habsburg claimant. Although the new Elector
of Brandenburg had a certain amount in common with the
Elector Palatine – they were brothers-in-law and Calvinists –
George William was cautious by nature, and with limited
resources and few troops at his disposal he was reluctant to
commit himself to Frederick's cause. Instead, he turned for
moral support to his neighbour, the Protestant Elector of
Saxony; it was the first step in a long-term dependency on
that state.

Many of George William's problems were inherited and not
of his own making. His territories were fragmented and without
effective communications or a common language, social structure or institutions. In Brandenburg–Prussia the nobility enjoyed
social and economic privileges conveyed by earlier margraves.
In Cleves–Mark and in Jülich (to which the Hohenzollerns
still claimed rights) the nobility was numerically smaller;
the peasants were for the most part tenants or free farmers and
there was a degree of urban independence in the many fortress

towns of the Rhine and Ruhr, administered by an efficient bureaucracy. Meanwhile, the core-state of Brandenburg was still comparatively poor. Its towns were small by western European standards and its commerce less developed. With a terrain of sandy heath interspersed with swamp, there was a natural shortage of fertile agricultural land and mineral deposits. The total population was about 270,000, considerably less than Prussia's 400,000; Berlin, the capital, had a mere 12,000 inhabitants. Despite being an electorate, Brandenburg–Prussia lacked the substance of a unified state. It was particularly vulnerable in time of war.

George William was an unsophisticated dynast. 'His policy was of a naked, dynastic simplicity; his only desire was that he should continue to be an Elector for all his days and that his son should succeed him' (16, pp. 221–2). With these objectives in mind he had to win the support of the Estates, and primarily of the great nobility, either by coercion or by soliciting their co-operation. On the whole the Prussian nobility and high officials were more accommodating than the junkers of Brandenburg, since it was in their interest, as it was in the Elector's, to exploit the affluent burghers in Prussia's thriving towns. The Estates granted taxes on a range of goods and services knowing that the townspeople would carry the major burden. In Cleves John Sigismund had already exploited old conflicts between the nobility and the towns to circumvent the Estates, levying indirect taxes on the transit and import of goods to the detriment of the Rhine trade. However, after 1621 George William's attempts to control the Estates of Cleves and Mark, and the Estates' efforts to defend their liberties against his government, foundered, as they were all caught up in the fighting between the forces of Spain and the United Provinces.

After the Spaniards occupied Jülich, Dutch troops invaded Cleves–Mark, ostensibly to protect the principality. These Dutch garrisons ignored the Estates, looting and forcibly extracting contributions and excise duties. To add insult to injury, the citizens had to contribute to the upkeep of the Elector's small army, even though it was incapable of protecting them. Undeterred, George William's officials forbade the Estates of Cleves–Mark to discuss policy matters or correspond with foreign states, and they also violated a customary privilege guaranteeing official appointments to local citizens. The Estates' resentment focused on the governor, Count Adam Schwartzenberg. In 1630 they threatened to appeal to the Emperor against their harsh treatment and in 1631 refused to co-operate until their grievances were redressed. As the Dutch occupation continued, the Estates defied the government and in 1637 formally protested against the treaty between Brandenburg and the United Provinces. Two years later the towns of Cleves repudiated a levy to help pay off the Dutch debt incurred under John Sigismund. But the struggle was evenly balanced. On some occasions the Estates of Cleves–Mark were forced to give way. In 1632, for example, the diet conceded taxes of 100,000 thalers, and in 1633 they failed to win government recognition of their right of free assembly.

The Elector believed that in Schwartzenberg he had found an ideal chief minister to counter the Estates and manipulate power in his princely interests. The count, who had served the Emperor as well as the dukes of Cleves, had no ties with the nobility of Brandenburg–Prussia, and to browbeat the junkers he resorted to the arbitrary methods which he had used in Cleves. After a celebrated treason case in 1627, he removed three noble members from the Privy Council and proceeded to sideline the institution by creating a new organ of government, the *Kriegsrat* or War Council, in 1630. Staffed by commoners or by foreign nobility, this body steadily took on other functions. By 1640 the Privy Council had effectively ceased to function.

In the interests of the Elector, Schwartzenberg now moved against the customary privileges of the Brandenburgers. The Estates were suspicious of George William's Calvinism; when they showed reluctance to advance him money, the minister's solution was to ignore their right of consent. Once the diet, the assembly of the Estates, had been dissolved, taxes were simply levied by force. As in Cleves, the Brandenburg Estates tried to strike back. The diet of 1636 refused to vote taxes until the accounts of the War Council had been handed over to them for scrutiny, but Schwartzenberg countered with the charge that the Estates' representative had failed to attend the *Kriegsrat*. By his determination and guile – qualities the Elector lacked – Schwartzenberg had forced the Estates into compliance by 1639. This point is often overlooked. It is usually George William's successors who are credited with breaking the particularism –

that is, the pursuit of vested rights – of the Estates in the interests of the absolute state. In fact, the process was under way before 1640.

However, the Thirty Years War imposed massive strains on Brandenburg–Prussia. Unlike Maximilian of Bavaria, who had amassed a large treasury and standing army before 1618, George William had no reserves, financial or military. By forced contributions it proved possible to raise the total militia from a negligible number to about 4,500 by 1640, but it was also necessary to resort to hiring mercenaries, so that discipline frequently broke down, epecially when Brandenburg became a theatre of war. For princes and generals of outstanding ability the war brought cash, provisions and services extracted from the defeated citizens. But it was George William's misfortune to have no military talent, and the most capable Brandenburg-born general, Hans Georg von Arnim, took service with more ambitious rulers, such as the Emperor and the Elector of Saxony. With no military reputation, Brandenburg–Prussia was a natural prey to aggressors. The imperialist general, Wallenstein, seized hostages in the Old Mark, demanding provisions and taxes from the townspeople of this western part of Brandenburg. In 1626 Gustavus Adolphus of Sweden captured Prussia's ports and siphoned off the proceeds of the Baltic trade. Five years later the Swedish army occupied most of Brandenburg, insisting on a monthly maintenance payment of 30,000 thalers from the inhabitants. Despite formal protests, Dutch garrisons extracted 1,500,000 thalers from the people of Cleves over a period of twenty-five years. The impoverishment and devastation affected all sections of society, including the landowning nobility. Tax grants could not be collected in full. George William was reduced to selling or mortgaging part of his estates. By 1640 a futile cycle of diminishing returns was in place.

International relations 1620–40

George William's main concern was to retain his patrimony. He was a conventional and conservative prince with a traditional respect for the Empire and its constitution as the embodiment of German liberties and the integrity of the states. Instinctively loyal to the Emperor, his first inclination and strategy in international affairs was to support imperial policy, or at least to avoid taking any serious step which would jeopardize it. The defeat and humiliation of Frederick of Bohemia, the 'Winter King', showed the consequences of defying the Habsburg Emperor. In fact, George William remained faithful to the imperial alliance for a decade, although his faith was often shaken by the Emperor's behaviour, and in particular by his decision to allow troops of Spain and the Catholic League to seize the Palatinate and occupy Cleves–Jülich (1620–3), to place Frederick under the imperial ban and then divest him of his title and principality in favour of the ambitious prince of Bavaria.

Both George William and John George of Saxony refused to recognize the validity of these last measures. They talked of raising a new Protestant Union of princes against the Catholic League. But their nerve failed, and in an act of gesture-politics, they made formal representations to the Emperor instead. Then, in 1626, after the imperial general Tilly had defeated the Protestant king of Denmark, George William took defensive precautions by renewing his loyalty to Ferdinand. But professions of allegiance were not enough to save him from a rap over the knuckles from his imperial overlord: Brandenburg was invaded by imperialist troops under Wallenstein. As a result, George William was too cowed to protest at the Emperor's unconstitutional dismissal of the Duke of Mecklenburg and the elevation of Wallenstein to his duchy (1627). He also turned a blind eye to the Emperor's growing ambition to extend imperial control into the Baltic.

It was the Edict of Restitution of 1629 which forced Brandenburg and Saxony to reconsider their loyalty to the Emperor. Ferdinand II revealed his deep hostility to Calvinism and threatened the strict enforcement of the clauses in the Peace of Augsburg safeguarding Catholic benefices. George William was alarmed that Protestants would lose their secularized lands. Ignoring the advice of Schwartzenberg, who was a Catholic, he joined his fellow Protestant princes in issuing a manifesto in 1630 criticizing the Restitution Edict. However, Ferdinand was at the height of his power and George William was always a reluctant rebel. His gesture made, he ultimately followed Saxony and tamely accepted the terms of the Peace of Prague in 1635. The new treaty still omitted a guarantee for Calvinism. It also enhanced the Emperor's authority at the expense of the princes and the Estates by binding them to supply troops to the imperialist army. Another clause, preventing the German princes from maintaining private armies, was shortly to leave Brandenburg at the mercy of another foreign invasion and occupation (1636–7).

If George William hoped to defend his fragmented territories by allegiance to the Emperor, his second strategy was to avoid military intervention by adopting a neutral position. His mistake was to confuse neutrality with appeasement: leaders such as Wallenstein and Gustavus Adolphus seized the opportunity to ride roughshod over his lands. It was, as the English agent Sir Thomas Roe observed at the time, 'too cold and stupid a neutrality'. He was neither machiavellian enough to exploit non-alignment, as the French did, nor intelligent enough to respond to changing situations. Neutrality did not save Cleves–Mark or the Prussian ports from foreign occupation; and although George William had kept out of the Danish–Saxon war (1625–6), Brandenburg suffered in Wallenstein's retaliatory campaigns (1626–7). Even as late as 1631, with the Swedes entrenched in nearby Pomerania, the Elector hesitated to abandon his neutral position. His failure to act left the way open for imperial troops to reach Magdeburg, and they sacked the city. Finally, after the Swedes stormed Frankfurt and appeared at the gates of Berlin George William's hand was forced. They had taken over all his fortresses except Küstrin on the Oder, leaving him with no choice in 1631 but to abandon his neutrality and side with the Swedish king. But he remained a reluctant ally and was wary of joining the Protestant union of German states, the League of Heilbronn (1633). After Sweden's defeat by the Imperialists at Nördlingen in 1634, he wavered, and in 1635, as we have seen, he turned back to the Emperor's cause, although his country paid dearly for this belated act of loyalty. In 1636 the military tables were turned once more against the Emperor and his allies at the battle of Wittstock-on-Dosse in northern Brandenburg. The Swedes occupied the electorate, exploiting its resources for the next eight years.

George William's dynastic connections proved to be another liability. He was tied by a web of Protestant marriage alliances to leading Calvinist dynasties as well as to the Lutheran House of Vasa. His wife was Elizabeth Charlotte of the Palatine, sister of the ill-fated 'Winter King' and a granddaughter of the great Protestant protagonist, William the Silent. The Elector's eldest sister was married to Gustavus Adolphus; another sister to Bethlen Gabor, the Calvinist Prince of Transylvania. A family pact also provided for the Hohenzollern succession to Pomerania on the death of Duke Bogislav XIV. Yet far from bringing protection to Brandenburg, these dynastic connections put added strains on George William's foreign policy. After the Bohemian débâcle and the expulsion of Frederick V and his family in 1620, George William felt bound to provide refuge for his Palatine in-laws and put at risk his professed neutrality. His chivalry brought him few thanks and no advantage, and it was a relief when they moved on to The Hague. However, his other brother-in-law, Bethlen Gabor, supported Frederick and campaigned against the Habsburgs in 1624 and 1626, placing George William's troubled relations with the Emperor in further jeopardy.

Meanwhile, his Orange and Vasa connections lulled him into a false sense of security. The Dutch proved to be predators, and Swedish self-interest proved far stronger than dynastic obligations. In three campaigns in 1626, 1631 and 1636–7, the Swedes occupied large areas of Brandenburg and the Baltic coastline of Prussia, yet this did not preclude a Swedish proposal that the Electoral Prince Frederick William should marry Gustavus Adolphus's only child, Christina. The last humiliation at the hands of Sweden came when the Duke of Pomerania died in 1637 and Swedish troops invaded the duchy despite George William's legitimate claim to the succession. Unable to expel them, the Elector retired to the relative security of Prussia, where he died in 1640. His legacy was mixed. His son and heir was strong, ambitious and able, but his patrimony was weak. 'Pomerania is lost, Jülich is lost, we hold Prussia like an eel by the tail, and we must mortgage the (Brandenburg) Mark', one of his advisors lamented.

The apprenticeship of Frederick William I 1640–48

The new Elector, Frederick William I (1620–88) was only 20 years old and was inexperienced in government and in military command. Yet he quickly decided that neither appeasement nor the imperial alliance had served Brandenburg–Prussia's interests. What his territories needed urgently was peace: not a humiliating peace imposed by foreign powers, but a negotiated peace that respected the territorial integrity and legal claims of his patrimony. It was logical that one of his first actions was to travel to Warsaw to receive formal recognition of his rights to the duchy of Prussia from the Polish king.

In Prussia Frederick William worked out his strategy. Against the advice of Schwartzenberg (whose opposition was anyway cut short by his death in 1641), he decided to break away from the imperial alliance. He halved his small mercenary army to stop the drain on his resources and indicate his conciliatory intentions, and he opened secret armistice negotiations with Sweden. From 1643, when Frederick William returned to Berlin to take control of the government, his aims became clear. He knew that the evacuation of Swedish troops was a precondition of Brandenburg's financial and material recovery. Preliminaries to an armistice had been signed in July 1641 but the Swedes continued to procrastinate. He realized that by reducing his forces he had sent out the wrong signals. Keen to retrench his position, he began to rearm in 1643–4, drawing on the manpower of Cleves, Prussia and Brandenburg to create a standing army of about 5,500 men. This included an elite personal bodyguard of 500 musketeers.

He was also helped by changes in Sweden. The ruler, Queen Christina, made clear her desire for peace. The armistice between Brandenburg and Sweden was finally ratified in 1644. The Swedes handed over some fortresses still in their possession, such as Frankfurt-on-Oder and Krossen. In the meantime, hostilities had again broken out in 1643 between Sweden and Denmark as the former overran Jutland. The Swedish government invited Frederick William to mediate in the dispute. The Peace of Brömsebro (1645) gave a certain boost to the young Elector's morale and reputation. Saxony, which for two decades had given the lead to George William, now followed Brandenburg's example in leaving the imperial alliance and concluding an armistice with Sweden.

Any general peace settlement, however, had to deal with many long-standing issues. Frederick William had already decided that the constitution of the German Empire was out of date. At the Diet of Regensburg (1640–41) he had given notice of his intention to leave the imperial alliance and repudiate the terms of the Peace of Prague as a basis for negotiating a general peace. He also took over the leadership of the Protestant cause, insisting that a settlement should protect Calvinists as well as Lutherans and that this should be reflected in the final distribution of land. His own ambitions were focused on certain territories to which he felt he had strong legal claims. He had firm expectations of winning Jülich and Berg from the Duke of Neuburg, in addition to retaining Cleves, Mark and Ravensburg. He also felt he had impeccable rights to Pomerania, which would guarantee Brandenburg–Prussia's position as a principal Baltic power. To emphasize this point he added to his objectives possession of the port of Stettin, the natural outlet for Brandenburg and Pomerania.

The Elector knew that his capabilities would be enhanced if he could rely on the support of the various Estates in his principalities. The death of Schwartzenberg was seen as an opportunity to re-establish harmonious relations. In 1640 the Brandenburg Estates petitioned him to govern moderately. One of his first actions had been the dissolution of the War Council and the restitution of the Privy Council, which he staffed with members of the Brandenburg and Pomeranian nobility. The restored *Geheimer Rat* was made responsible for military matters. The new Elector had made a decision to rule with the help of the junker class; until general peace was restored it was politic to keep on good terms with the Estates of Brandenburg–Prussia.

He was less cautious in his handling of the Estates of Cleves–Mark, which were a useful source of men and money supplies. The burgher representatives in the Estates resented the exemption of the nobility from taxation. They also opposed an Electoral policy of granting special 'jurisdictions' to favoured nobles, which gave them wide police and judicial powers over the inhabitants of certain villages and estates in return for substantial payments to the Elector's coffers. In 1649 he had to concede to the Cleves Estates that in future jurisdictions would only be granted with their consent. But meanwhile, Frederick William had aroused their anger on another issue. In 1646 the Elector's troops attacked the principality of Berg. The Estates of Cleves–Mark protested, and their resistance to electoral efforts to levy the necessary taxation contributed to the failure of the attempted coup. The Elector's actions also united all four Estates of Cleves, Jülich, Mark and Berg in solidarity together.

In 1649 Frederick William had to make sweeping concessions to the Estates, some of them – such as the right to free assembly and free negotiation with foreign powers, and the dismissal of foreign officials – the very rights which his father George William had removed.

The attempted seizure of Berg had been part of the Elector's plan to put pressure on the Dutch to support his claim to the territories of Jülich–Berg. His evacuation of Berg was sealed by his marriage to the Princess Louise Henriette (1646), renewing the Hohenzollerns' old ties with the house of Orange. However, Frederick William's hopes that Dutch influence would be decisive in furthering his territorial aims were dashed. The Jülich–Berg dispute rumbled on, and for some years Dutch and Spanish troops remained in occupation of key fortresses.

At the negotiations held in the Westphalian towns of Osnabrück and Münster (1644–8) all the participants tried to negotiate advantages for their states, while prolonging the fighting in Germany. Frederick William, as self-interested as the rest, took the opportunity of Poland's weakness to arrogate to himself all the port dues of Pillau and Memel (1646), which he claimed as the Duke of Prussia. In the final peace settlement, however, he had to forgo his aim of securing Stettin from Sweden. As to his other claim, Pomerania, he realized he had no option but to compromise. He received the poorer region of East Pomerania, while Sweden took the richer, western half. By way of compensation Frederick William secured the secularized bishoprics of Halberstadt, Minden and Kammin and the right to take possession of the archbishopric of Magdeburg on the death of its administrator. He could view these gains with satisfaction, given his abject bargaining position in 1640.

Redressing the balance?

The reign of Elector George William is frequently presented as a nadir in the development of Brandenburg–Prussia, the dark of weakness and defeat before the dawn of modern absolutism under Frederick William. This interpretation owes much to Samuel Pufendorf, chief publicist to Frederick William, whose propaganda disparaged what went before in order to bolster his patron's achievements. As a version of events it is somewhat misleading. George William was certainly timid and indecisive and he had few diplomatic or military gifts. His son, on the other hand, known to his contemporaries and posterity alike as the Great Elector, was a bold and effective opportunist. However, posterity has perhaps focused too sharply on the contrasting personalities of father and son and overlooked the degree of continuity in their problems and policies. They had to manage on limited economic resources and exercise political authority while taking account of the traditional rights of the Estates. War forced both rulers into political mistakes. George William inherited a truculent nobility and the problem of defending and controlling isolated territories without a state army. He handed on these problems to Frederick William. However, in two respects he also showed his successor the way. As a convinced dynast, George William would not relinquish his claim to succeed to the duchy of Pomerania, and though forced to accept the Swedish military occupation, he conveyed an obdurate belief to Frederick William that possession should be a prerequisite of peace. In addition, during his reign, his chief minister, Schwartzenberg, took the initiative against the Estates, creating a precedent for establishing autocratic government.

George William was a malleable prince. He believed in German liberties but was restrained throughout his reign by the prevailing respect for the imperial authority, forcibly exercised by Ferdinand II. It is equally clear that Frederick William gained from the new international climate. By 1640 a general war-weariness had set in across Europe. The generation of brilliant military commanders, from Spinola to Wallenstein and Gustavus Adolphus, who had humbled the German states in the 1620s, was dead. As Duke of Prussia, Frederick William had little to fear from the tolerant king of Poland, and in diplomatic circles Emperor Ferdinand III was increasingly isolated. Frederick William was astute enough to benefit from this change.

2

The Great Elector
Foreign relations and policies 1648–88

The aftermath of Westphalia 1648–54

The negotiations in Westphalia led to a period of uneasy peace. The treaty of Osnabrück increased the territorial strength of Brandenburg–Prussia on paper, but the terms had to be implemented before Frederick William I could be satisfied with his gains. His possessions were still scattered from the Rhine to the Niemen. He was annoyed by his failure to win recognition of his claim to Jülich–Berg. From his point of view Stettin would have been vastly preferable to the East Pomeranian port of Kolberg or the bishopric of Kammin. His newly-won province of East Pomerania was separated from East Prussia by a broad Polish corridor, and the principalities of Hanover and Brunswick stood between Minden and the Old Mark of Brandenburg. The acquisition of Halberstadt was certainly gratifying in that it fulfilled a century-old Hohenzollern ambition, but possession of Magdeburg, promising control of the main Elbe crossing, had to wait until the death of its bishop-administrator, which did not occur until 1680.

Although the peace effectively confirmed the sovereignty of the German princes, Frederick William found that in reality a prince's independence was proportionate to his military might. He was frustrated by his inability to get what he wanted, even when he could claim violations of Westphalia. For instance, in

1651 he found he had to call on the Emperor to mediate in the matter of the Jülich–Berg dispute. Despite undertakings made in 1614 and 1647, the Catholic Count-Palatine of Neuburg, his rival claimant for the duchies, continued to persecute the Protestant inhabitants of Berg. Such religious intolerance defied the spirit of Westphalia, and this provided Frederick William with the pretext he wanted to launch a second invasion of Jülich–Berg. It was a military blunder, and when the operation failed he was only saved from a humiliating climb-down by Ferdinand III's intervention (1651). Yet on this, as on other occasions, the Elector made the best of a bad situation. By promising to support the Emperor's son in his quest for the title of King of the Romans, he persuaded Ferdinand to put pressure on Sweden to fulfil its obligations under the Treaty of Osnabrück.

It was a matter of concern to Brandenburg that Sweden, by gaining West Pomerania and the bishoprics of Bremen and Verden at the Peace of Westphalia, was confirmed in control of the lower Weser, Elbe and Oder rivers. However, the delays in implementing the peace settlement and Sweden's prevarication on the removal of its armed forces greatly aggravated feeling. The details of land transfer and boundary changes were not settled until 1650, by the supplementary Treaty of Nürnberg; the precise division of Pomerania was only agreed finally by the Treaty of Stettin (1653) and it was another year before the Swedes evacuated East Pomerania. Even then, to the Elector's chagrin, half the customs revenues of East Pomeranian towns were the prerogative of Sweden. Furthermore, as a guarantor of Westphalia, Sweden was in a strong position to intervene in disputes arising from the settlement, including those relating to individual princes of the Empire.

Brandenburg and the first Nordic War 1655–60

As Frederick William finally took possession of East Pomerania, his interest in the Baltic intensified. In 1654 Queen Christina of Sweden abdicated in favour of her cousin, Charles X. The new king showed every sign of emulating Gustavus Adolphus in his desire to make the Baltic a Swedish lake. The Elector was alerted to the prospect of another war between Sweden and Poland when Charles approached him with a demand for the towns of

Pillau and Memel as the price of a Swedish–Brandenburg alliance (1654). Frederick William was reluctant to make quick concessions even to gain a powerful ally. He was wary of being drawn into another conflict which might result in the loss of his hard-won Westphalian gains; but more to the point, his instinct was to secure the maximum advantage from the situation by selling his military support to the highest bidder. Meanwhile, to protect his own position he turned to the Dutch Republic, whose vital trading interests would also be affected by Swedish occupation of the Baltic ports. A defensive treaty was concluded at The Hague in 1655, by which the Elector hoped to retain his independence.

However, within a matter of weeks Sweden's armies swept across the plains of Poland, capturing all the leading cities. They then wheeled round against Polish Prussia, and after taking all the towns except Danzig, moved on to the duchy of Prussia. Backed into a corner at Königsberg, the Elector avoided battle to save his army and accepted the Swedish terms (1656). Charles X appeared to have brought Brandenburg–Prussia to heel. Ducal Prussia became a Swedish fief and Frederick William promised military and financial aid to his overlord, and the use of Pillau and Memel, along with half the port dues. As a modest reward to his new vassal, Charles allowed Frederick William to take the bishopric of Ermland, an enclave within East Prussia.

The Treaty of Königsberg (1656) exemplified the Elector's dilemma. Armed neutrality was an obvious strategy for a second-class state, but there would be situations in which the ruler would be forced to take sides. By arming his state in order to sell its military capacity, he had to ask himself whether it was better to take the initiative and negotiate with the superior power in the hope of winning an ally's prize. Or was it wiser to support the weaker of two major powers in the expectation that the aggressor would eventually be defeated by a hostile coalition? Over the years Frederick William turned to both these strategies and switched from one alliance to another. If he was flexible and inconsistent in his diplomatic and military strategies, he was unwavering in his overall objective, which was to enhance his possessions and the status of the dynasty he embodied. This impelled him to take every possible step to defend and consolidate his patrimony.

Later in 1656, as the Poles recovered much of their lost

ground, the Elector found himself courted by both sides. But it was too early to desert Sweden, which still appeared the dominant power. In return for a promise of territorial booty in the west of Poland, he agreed by the Treaty of Marienburg (1656) to fight alongside the Swedes. Leading his army of 8,500 troops, Frederick William joined in the three-day battle of Warsaw, where he proved his military prowess. The victory caused Sweden's enemies to re-form. The Dutch fleet came to the defence of Danzig, the Russians took Ingria and Livonia and Ferdinand III sent help to John Casimir, the Polish king. Frederick William saw his chance to turn the diplomatic tables on his ally, Sweden. He had also clarified his war aims, for the war had already shown how elusive territorial gains and promises could be. But there was an important constitutional matter to be rectified: the Elector wanted to be freed permanently from Swedish and Polish suzerainty. In the Treaty of Labiau (1656) Charles X agreed to this demand and recognized Frederick William as the sovereign ruler of ducal Prussia. In addition, Sweden surrendered her claims to the customs dues levied in Prussian ports. With these concessions secured, a small Brandenburg force joined in Charles's latest campaign against Poland (1657).

The hostilities in Poland, however, turned into an inconclusive guerilla campaign. When Denmark declared war against Sweden and Charles X decided to decamp from the mainland to concentrate on fighting his oldest enemy, Brandenburg returned to a state of armed neutrality. To conserve his army, Frederick William withdrew circumspectly into Prussia (1657). Sweden was now on the defensive against a coalition of powers and Frederick William no longer felt the need for the Swedish alliance. Charles X's departure and Poland's relative weakness gave him an opportunity to make further political capital. He expressed his readiness to come to terms with the Poles on the key condition which he had won from the Swedes at Labiau: recognition of his sovereignty in Prussia. As it happened, the Emperor had his own dynastic reasons for wanting to detach Brandenburg from the Swedish alliance. In the ensuing negotiations he put pressure on the Polish king to match the Swedish bid and accept Frederick William's sovereign rights over ducal Prussia. In the Treaty of Wehlau (1657) John Casimir reluctantly made this substantial concession, and in return Brandenburg returned Ermland to Poland. Frederick William followed this triumph with a total turnabout when he agreed terms with the Austrian Emperor and the King of Denmark.

By 1658 the Nordic War was in its last phase. The fighting had concentrated on Denmark, where the spectacular gains made by Charles X in 1657 were partly countered by the armies of the anti-Swedish coalition, to which Frederick William contributed a Brandenburg force. The possibility of territorial gains at Sweden's expense now opened up. At the head of 30,000 men, the Elector drove the Swedes from Schleswig and Holstein (1658) before turning his attention to Swedish Pomerania and the ports of Stralsund and Stettin in particular. Although Stettin withstood his attacks, by the end of 1659 Brandenburg forces were in control of most of Pomerania. In the event of peace, the Elector's bargaining position against Sweden looked stronger than it had ever been. His main goal was Swedish Pomerania, which he had failed to achieve at Westphalia.

It was the intervention of another superior power which blocked Frederick William's strategy. The French minister, Mazarin, was reluctant to see Sweden lose her prime position in the Baltic. Brandenburg's allies in the anti-Swedish coalition – Poland, Denmark and the Austrian Emperor – had grown weary of the war, despite the fact that Sweden's position was suddenly weakened by the death of Charles X (1660) and the advent of a regency for his 4-year-old son. However, Frederick William learned again the harsh reality of politics, that a second-rate power is unwise to abandon neutrality and fight alone. At the Peace of Oliva (1660) the Elector's recent allies had no reason to support him against French diplomacy, which carried the day. He had to accept a compromise. He secured his first war aim, the recognition by all the signatories that he was the sovereign Duke of Prussia. But to his deep disappointment he had to withdraw his army from western Pomerania and accept Sweden's possession of the Baltic province.

Defence of the status quo 1658–67

As the Nordic War drew to a close, Frederick William's attention concentrated again on events in Germany. Here the general concern for a settled period of peace was the main surety for the Westphalian settlement. However, many German princes still saw the power of Emperor Ferdinand III as a potential source of danger to the political balance, and there was a broad desire to take appropriate precautions. It suited Frederick William to play on this perception, encouraged by his Calvinist minister, the Count of Waldeck, a petty sovereign prince in his own right. The Elector gave his support to Waldeck's plan for a defensive union of the Protestant princes and Estates (1654). In response, a counter-alliance was formed (1655) by the Archbishop-Elector of Cologne to protect the rights of the Catholic princes. The death of Ferdinand III two years later and the election of his second son, Leopold, to the imperial title gave the princes an opportunity to serve a further warning to the Emperor. In 1658 the Archbishop of Mainz, one of the three ecclesiastical electors, sponsored the formation of another union, the League of the Rhine (*Rheinbund*), which pledged its princely members to give mutual military support against internal and external enemies. However, Frederick William was mistrustful of the architects of the League (which included Mazarin's agent, the French ambassador). He also questioned whether the league would safeguard the peace, so he delayed joining for as long as he could.

The Elector had always made it clear that he interpreted the legal claims of the Hohenzollerns as inalienable rights, so that in defending his territorial claims he was defending the political status quo in northern Europe. For this reason he believed he was quite justified in launching attacks on Jülich–Berg in 1646 and 1651, even though he was labelled a warmonger. In fact, an official state of peace was not a deterrent to ambitious princes; they would still resort to military action if they believed it would achieve their political ends. In 1664 the army of the Rhineland league reduced the town of Erfurt at the request of the Archbishop of Mainz. In 1666 the Swedish Regency forcibly ordered the port of Bremen to take an oath of allegiance; only a warning of armed opposition by Denmark, the United Provinces and Brandenburg persuaded the Swedes to back down. In the same year, as war loomed between the Catholic prince-bishop of Münster and the Dutch Republic, the situation was saved partly by Frederick William's threat to send an army from Cleves in defence of the Dutch. In the midst of this, the Elector himself forced an armed garrison on the city of Magdeburg as a guarantee of his rights of reversion, granted in 1648. At the same time he settled his quarrel with the ruler of Neuburg, surrendering his claim to Jülich–Berg to ensure his sovereign rights over Cleves, Mark and Ravensberg. By force and negotiation he was tidying up some of the loose ends arising from the Peace of Westphalia.

It was becoming apparent by the 1660s that if the status quo was in danger, the threat would come not from the Emperor Leopold but from France. Louis XIV was determined to take the Spanish Netherlands in the name of his Spanish wife, Maria Theresa, whose claim rested on an ancient right of devolution. He was confident that the German princes in the League of the Rhine would not hinder his plans when, in the spring of 1667, French armies swept into Flanders. The *Rheinbund* dissolved in disarray and Frederick William, conscious of France's predominance in Europe, tried unsuccessfully to persuade the German princes to form an anti-Bourbon coalition. But Louis knew how to play on the Elector's blatant self-interest. While the main Protestant states, Sweden, the United Provinces and England, were negotiating the Triple Alliance (Janury 1668) to bring pressure on France, Frederick William was effectively bribed by Louis to sign the Treaty of Berlin (1667), by which he agreed to remain neutral and turn a blind eye to French advances. The consequent gains made by France in the War of Devolution encouraged Louis to believe that the territorial boundaries of the Peace of Westphalia were no longer valid.

Brandenburg and the changing balance of power 1668–88

After Louis XIV's lightning destruction of the Spanish Netherlands in 1667–8, other states followed Frederick William's example of non-aggression towards France. Charles II of England signed a secret treaty with the French king in 1670, and Emperor Leopold's secret partition agreement in 1668 was succeeded by a treaty of neutrality three years later. The Palatinate and Wurttemberg also declared themselves neutral, while Cologne and Münster went so far as to align with France. This left Louis free to plan his next onslaught against the Dutch. However, as the Elector observed the preliminaries – the French occupation of Lorraine and Cologne – he began to change his mind about the wisdom of colluding with France. He reasoned that if the French were to seize hold of the Dutch Republic, not only the commerce of the Rhinelands but his own sovereignty in Cleves and Mark would be in jeopardy. So with calculated boldness he signed an alliance with the Dutch, bargaining the use of 20,000 soldiers in return for half their maintenance costs and the belated evacuation of the Dutch garrisons from Cleves and Mark. In the event, this volte-face was another miscalculation. At the opening of the Dutch War in 1672, Brandenburg could not stop the French army marching through Cleves, nor could the Elector save the desperate Dutch government from suing for peace. When a half-hearted attempt to muster Austro-Brandenburg forces against Louis petered out, the Elector hastily cut his losses. He concluded his own terms with Louis in the Peace of Vossem (1673), just as a new anti-French alliance of the Emperor, the Dutch and Spain was taking shape. Then, in another audacious but cynical stroke, he switched sides again because the promised French subsidies had failed to materialize; and he committed his troops to the allied forces based on the upper Rhine in 1674–5. This provocative act had repercussions: it brought France's ally, the youthful Charles XI of Sweden, into the war. At the end of 1674 the Swedish forces invaded Brandenburg.

The renewal of the northern conflict put paid to Frederick William's campaigning in Germany. After negotiating support with the Emperor, Denmark and the Dutch against Sweden, he brought his army of 15,000 men back to the Elbe, from where he launched a surprise attack on the Swedish base at Rathenow on the Havel. This was followed by a celebrated victory in the marshy lowlands north-west of Berlin. The battle of Fehrbellin in 1675 forced the Swedes back into Pomerania, and as Brandenburg's first unilateral triumph, it won for Frederick William the title of 'The Great Elector'. However, it was only the beginning of four years of gruelling warfare for the conquest of Western Pomerania. Although a Danish fleet took command of the Baltic, the Brandenburgers had to battle for possession of the province and its strongholds, Stettin, Stralsund and Greifswald (1678). Then a last-ditch attack by the Swedes tempted the Great Elector to go too far. In a winter campaign to head off an attack from Livonia, he led his army over the frozen waterways of Prussia towards the Vistula. Too late he learned of the diplomatic manoeuvrings of other states. The Dutch Republic, Spain and the Emperor had made peace with Louis XIV in 1678, and, unhindered, the next year the French army was able to threaten Minden which Frederick William had acquired in 1648. He was forced to settle again with Louis. Abandoning Denmark, his only remaining ally, he signed the Peace of Saint-Germain-en-Laye (1679). The all-powerful king of France ensured that the hard-won Pomeranian gains, including Stettin, were handed back to Sweden for a second time. Brandenburg was given a small concessionary strip on the right bank of the Oder and was allowed to keep the tolls levied in its own territory of East Pomerania.

The Dutch War convinced Frederick William that the balance of power had irretrievably tipped in favour of France. Only by soliciting French help would he win Swedish Pomerania. He was in any case disillusioned with the Emperor. In 1675 Leopold had blocked his inheritance of three small territories in Silesia, Liegnitz, Brieg and Wohlau (in addition to an earlier claim to Jägernsdorf), pronouncing them dependencies of the Bohemian crown. In 1679 the Great Elector concluded a secret alliance with Louis XIV, allowing the French free passage through his lands in return for an annual pension of 100,000 livres and a ten-year guarantee of his sovereignty. This understanding survived the growing anger towards France in Germany and Sweden during the early 1680s, a hostility caused by Louis XIV's arbitrary *réunion* policy of seizing the dependent lands of past French conquests.

By 1685, however, even Frederick William saw that French expansionism had reached menacing levels. The threat to Protestantism posed by Louis' repeal of the Edict of Nantes in 1685 and the danger to the Rhine states was such that he once more decided to jettison his French ally. He had calculated that it was better to sacrifice his claim to West Pomerania to ensure the security of his existing territories, especially if they were guaranteed by a network of alliances. His last diplomatic manoeuvres included the renewal of his alliance with his nephew, William of Orange (1685), a defensive pact with his former enemy, Charles XI of Sweden (1686) and a secret defensive alliance with Emperor Leopold (1686). He had already sent a Brandenburg contingent to support the Emperor in his war with the Turks (1683–4). Now he was ready to negotiate further with Leopold; in return for military co-operation and subsidies, and the acquisition of the small enclave of Schwiebus, he would give up his claims to the Silesian territories. By 1688 he was calmly awaiting William III's seizure of the English throne and the consequent inclusion of England in the great anti-French coalition.

A state to reckon with?

In the welter of Frederick William's diplomatic and military activity, it is important not to exaggerate his achievements but to weigh them against his objectives. As a military leader he was tenacious and bold, but he could never be classed with Gustavus Adolphus, Wallenstein or Turenne. His abilities put him on a par with other German princes – Elector Max Emanuel of Bavaria, Charles Duke of Lorraine or Margrave Ludwig of Baden – all of whom made their military reputations fighting the Turks. Fehrbellin, the battle which earned Frederick William historic fame, was certainly no classic victory, for the Swedes were able to conduct an orderly retreat. There is no doubt that he was capable of military and diplomatic errors of judgement. His tendency to treat alliances as matters of crude expediency tarnished his reputation abroad and earned him few friends. 'The most cunning fox of Europe' was the verdict of one French diplomat. His initial aim, the survival of Brandenburg–Prussia, had been achieved by 1648, as the universal exhaustion of participants in the Thirty Years War worked to his advantage.

In the Westphalia settlement French and Swedish determination to weaken the Empire saved Brandenburg–Prussia and held out to Frederick William territorial gains which he could not have hoped for at his accession. On the other hand, when his ambitions appeared excessive, as they did at the Oliva negotiations (1660), he was thwarted by Franco-Swedish solidarity. In fact, by 1660 his main achievements in foreign policy were behind him. Later successes – the Dutch evacuation of Cleves–Mark (1672) or his accession to Magdeburg (1680) – followed on from earlier negotiations. The Schwiebus agreement proved an empty gain, since the Electoral Prince made a secret pact to return it to the Emperor. In 1688 the Great Elector still took a patrimonial view of the patchwork of territories bound to him by dynastic ties. The unification of those lands into a single, coextensive state was **not** yet a viable objective of Hohenzollern foreign policy.

What the Elector Frederick William did achieve was a notable enhancement of his dynasty's prestige. He was the ruler of a state to be reckoned with, a prince with whom European sovereigns were ready to negotiate. In the course of his long reign he established Brandenburg–Prussia as a pivotal power in Europe on the basis of its being a credible, efficient military machine. By 1688 his army was estimated to be 30,000 strong. This was the key to his concept of security in international affairs. 'Alliances, to be sure, are good, but forces of one's own still better', wrote the Great Elector in 1667. In this respect he set Brandenburg–Prussia in a new direction.

3

The Great Elector: internal reconstruction 1648–88

Elector Frederick William I was driven by a will to succeed. His stern Calvinist faith drove him to build a state dedicated to order, a militaristic, bureaucratic regime, which would earn him widespread respect. The destruction of the Thirty Years War had brought about a general desire for stability and security which he was able to exploit. But for forty years he also used the recurrent threat of war to force change on his subjects and to undercut the traditional balance of power between the ruler and the Estates in favour of his own paternalistic government.

The armed forces and their administration

By 1648 Frederick William had learned the lesson that a standing army was a symbol of power and prestige, a key to political success. The army and its needs became the prime mover in all internal changes. In the first place, the size of the army steadily increased. By the end of the first Nordic War it had reached a total of 22,000 men, and although in the peacetime the numbers were reduced to 12,000 men, Dutch subsidies enabled the total to rise to 45,000 by the end of the Franco-Dutch War (1678); and at the Great Elector's death (1688) his peacetime army was still 30,000 strong. He was not afraid to borrow ideas from other countries which had pioneered achievements in military law, technology and tactics. In 1654–5 he adopted Dutch drill regulations for his troops and in 1656 took over Gustavus Adolphus's articles of war, the basis of Swedish military law. To ensure the firepower of the Brandenburg infantry, two-thirds had been equipped with the flintlock musket by the 1670s, leaving the remaining third as pikemen. (The bayonet was not officially introduced until 1689.) The army was among the first in Europe to introduce a uniform for all ranks, providing a sense of identity and contributing to good discipline on the battlefield.

The Great Elector's principal aim was to forge an efficient, disciplined, unified fighting force out of the mixture of European mercenaries and native-born peasantry who formed the rank and file. He took his own military role seriously; he led his troops personally in the campaign of 1674–5 in Alsace and at Fehrbellin. While retaining the command system of colonels and regiments, he insisted that recruitment was carried out in his name. All superior officers were engaged by the Elector himself, including Field-Marshal von Sparr, who served as his first Commander-in-Chief from 1655 to 1668, and Field-Marshal Derfflinger, a brilliant cavalry officer who had learned his skills in the Swedish army. To encourage a reliable officer class, a small military academy was set up at Kolberg in Pomerania to train some twenty to twenty-five officers a year. Although sons of native-born noblemen were favoured, the Elector rated talent more highly than social class. Under von Sparr a prototype of a military civil service or General Staff was developed, starting with the appointment in 1655 of Claus von Platen as the chief official, the General War Commissary (*Generalkriegskommissar*). His task was to administer the army with the help of a hierarchy of officials centred on a new institution, an all-powerful general War Office (*Generalkriegskommissariat*) in Berlin. He was therefore ultimately responsible for the recruitment, training, billeting, equipment and supplies of the armed forces and for raising the financial levies needed to pay and maintain them. In order to deal with this last important matter, a separate war treasury (*Generalkriegskasse*) was set up in 1674 to handle foreign subsidies and subsequently to deal with all forms of taxation. From 1679 the activities of the General War Commissariat were further extended by its new chief, Joachim Ernst von Grumbkow, who combined the functions of Chief of the General Staff and Ministers of War and Finance. Through his initiative almost every concern of government was concentrated in the central War Office, creating a regime that was essentially authoritarian and militarist.

By comparison, Frederick William's naval programme was modest. As a youth in Leyden, he had observed the economic effects of Dutch sea power, and later he was also impressed by Sweden's maritime control of the Baltic. Despite Brandenburg's landlocked position, he was convinced by a Dutch shipowner, Benjamin Raule, of both the strategic and the commercial advantages of a navy. Raule was given the task of hiring a fleet of twenty ships to sail under the Brandenburg flag, supported by the profits of privateering. To the Great Elector's satisfaction, the navy played a part in the capture of Stettin in the War of 1675–9, and in 1681 it also beat the Spaniards off Cape St Vincent.

Taxation policy and relations with the Estates

Support for a permanent standing army put a new financial burden on the state. Frederick William's prime objective was to regularize the funding of his armed forces. Hitherto there were four main sources of internal revenue: rents from the sovereign's domains, the *regalia* (river and road tolls, profits from mines and the mint), a direct land and poll tax, or *Contribution*, for the defence of the realm, from which the nobility was exempt, and, last, extraordinary taxes which the ruler could ask the Estates (*Landstände*) to grant as special subsidies. Since Brandenburg and the other territories were relatively poor in economic terms, there were limits as to how much could be raised. In wartime the Elector keenly sought foreign subsidies to boost his state income: in due course these contributed some 10 per cent of his military budget.

The revenue over which he had the most direct control was that of his own domains, although the Thirty Years War had caused depopulation and declining rents. Financial recovery was slow, but the Elector's answer was to administer the crown lands and collect their revenues through provincial chambers (*Amtskammer*). Money payments replaced payment in kind. Under an able and efficient director of finance, Freiherr von

Knyphausen, whom Frederick William appointed to head the embryonic central finance bureau (*Hofkammer*) in Brandenburg in 1684, a small profit of 125,000 thalers was raised from domain lands. The Elector also tried to impose new taxes. In 1651 he introduced a stamp duty without consulting the Brandenburg Estates, but had to back down. He also turned repeatedly to a tax on the Dutch model, the Excise duty on consumption, sales and the movement of goods, which he believed would be highly lucrative. The methods by which he attempted to increase revenue, alternately mollifying, forcibly squeezing, or compromising with his subjects, brought about a prolonged showdown. Yet, despite vigorous protests from the Diets (*Landtäge*), he managed to treble the annual state revenues to 3.4 million thalers.

In the aftermath of the Peace of Westphalia the Great Elector tried to win the co-operation of the Estates of Brandenburg. After resisting both his stamp duty (1651) and a proposed excise tax (1652), they put forward a list of grievances. Negotiations at the Brandenburg Diet finally resulted in a compromise agreement – the famous Recess of 1653 – by which the Elector secured a grant of 530,000 thalers payable by the burghers and commoners over six years; in return, the nobles' wide socio-economic privileges and the Estates' right to be consulted on the excise were confirmed. On this basis Frederick William was able to expand the army to 20,000 men, but when the agreed amount proved insufficient for the war years of 1655–7, he not only drastically increased it, using soldiers to enforce the levy, but also demanded supplies in kind to the same value. In 1667 a Diet was summoned to discuss the introduction of the excise on a range of services and goods (such as beer, wine, spirits, salt, seed-corn and cattle), to take effect in the towns for three years. The measure was not a success and most towns abandoned it in 1670. However, the burghers were not to get away so lightly. In 1680–2 the Elector ordered its re-imposition in the towns of Brandenburg. In the meantime, the duty was also imposed in the Elector's new territories of Pomerania, Magdeburg, Minden and Halberstadt. As for the lesser nobles, despite their exemption from the *Contribution*, Frederick William managed to extract 40 thalers from each fief in lieu of feudal war service.

In Cleves–Mark the Estates were more active in resisting electoral pressure. After winning far-reaching concessions and privileges from the Great Elector in 1649 and 1653, their position seemed secure, especially after the second Neuburg War of 1651. But with the outbreak of the Nordic War in 1655, Frederick William used the military emergency to enlist soldiers in Cleves–Mark and send in troops to extract subsidies by force, despite the protests of his governor. During the war years of 1655–60 1.5 million thalers were raised in the Rhineland states, and at the end of the war Frederick William threatened to revoke some of his earlier concessions. Using his personal authority to the full he forced the Estates to accept a clever compromise by the Recess of 1660–1. The *Landstände* were allowed to keep their right of free assembly and to vote and audit taxes, but in return they gave up other rights: those of negotiation with foreign powers, consent to the levy and maintenance of troops and the appointment and dismissal of officials, who henceforth took a personal oath to the Elector. With his powers strengthened, in 1664–5 the Elector forcibly raised a hearth tax on the towns of Cleves–Mark to help pay for troops reputedly needed to fight the Ottoman Turks. However, nine attempts by the Elector in the period 1667–87 to introduce the excise there failed. On the other hand, after his territorial settlement with the Duke of Neuburg (1666), the Estates of Cleves–Mark paid formal homage to Frederick William as their sovereign, indicating his success in bringing these lands under his administrative grip.

The situation in Prussia was somewhat different again. The relative goodwill between the Prussian Estates and Frederick William, their duke, came to an end with the Nordic War (1655–60). In the wartime emergency he collected taxes without the prior agreement of the Estates. The Prussian nobles, who aspired to the liberties of the Polish nobility, also complained about foreign officers in their regiments and the interference of the governor, Prince Radziwill. Resentment about levels of taxation and troop enlistment surfaced in the Diet of 1661–3. Although the nobles and wealthy burghers agreed to recognize Frederick William's sovereignty over Prussia in accordance with the Peace of Oliva (1660), the commoners of Königsberg refused. Frederick William reacted with customary firmness. The leader of the popular opposition, Hieronymus Roth, a prominent member of the Merchants' Guild, was arrested for treason in 1661 and imprisoned until his death in 1678. Meanwhile, the

Estates paid homage to their sovereign lord before the Diet closed in 1663. In response, Frederick William made some tactical concessions. He confirmed the Estates' privileges, promised not to levy taxes without their consent and allowed the citizens of Königsberg to raise their own taxes. In this way he secured the *Contribution* to maintain the army in peace time. From 1669, however, he reneged on his tax promises; as a result, the Estates refused to vote subsidies for the army's upkeep. Again, the Elector responded with force. Later, in 1674, Königsberg was subjected to an army of occupation with orders to extract the *Contribution*. Meanwhile, Frederick William broke the nobles' hostility to his policies by kidnapping one of their leaders, Christian von Kalckstein, who had gone to Warsaw to submit the protests of the Estates to the Polish Diet. Brought back to Prussia rolled in a carpet, von Kalckstein was tortured, tried and executed for treason in 1672. By the end of his reign the Prussian nobility had abandoned its opposition to the Great Elector.

Armed force was only one method by which the Estates were undermined. Meetings of the full Diets were already rare by 1652, but he defaulted on promises to summon them regularly and played on the rivalry and self-interest of the social classes on the basis of divide and rule. By the 1680s he had succeeded in separating the towns from the rural areas for taxation purposes and in splitting the classes of the Estates by negotiating with the noble representatives and subordinating the interests of the burghers and other non-noble representatives. This policy had constitutional implications; it contributed to the decline of the Estates and paved the way for absolute rule.

However, his crucial reform was to use military officials to take over civil matters. Generally officers administered areas where they had no personal links: Colonel von Barfuss, for example, a Brandenburger, was sent to lead the Prussian Commissariat. Since the army was the largest consumer of state revenues, it seemed logical to give the task of assessing and collecting taxes, including the *Contribution* and later the excise, to the military officers of the *Generalkriegskommissariat*. The billeting of troops, once a function of the Estates, was taken over by the military authorities. Under von Grumbkow the process was carried to extremes. He and his officers were ruthless in their dedication to the Elector's interests. After 1680 the General War Commissariat also handled a range of economic matters, including tax reform, and finally they began to supervise traditional urban officials, such as aldermen, and take control of the entire municipal administration of the principalities.

This was true at the highest as well as at the local level. The Privy Council (*Geheimer Rat*), which Frederick William had revived in 1640, was placed in the trusted hands of Otto von Schwerin, who became President in 1658. It served as the highest judicial court and the central administrative body for all the electoral territories. But after Schwerin's death in 1679 it was gradually deprived of its competence over matters such as petitions, financial, military and territorial affairs. Friction between the privy councillors and the heads of the General War Commissariat simmered for two decades from 1660, while the Elector increasingly vested power in a Secret Council, which met two or three times a week and became the central organ of government. After 1680 von Grumbkow ensured that the function of the Privy Council became merely consultative. By 1688 the military bureaucracy dominated the civil service and government.

The impact of administrative change on the social structure

The revolts of 1661 and 1672 in Prussia constituted the only serious opposition to Elector Frederick William's policies. In the other principalities, his opponents fought the struggle with words, while he manipulated them using soldiers. By agreeing to a compromise, such as the 1653 Recess, he was able to secure the taxation he needed in return for confirming old privileges and granting additional rights to the nobility over matters of seigneurial jurisdiction. An alliance of self-interest was forged between the prince and the nobility. While the junkers were not exempt from taxation, their burden was far lighter than that of other classes. The Great Elector was also able to harness the nobility to state service by drawing them into the officer corps of the army or the military bureaucracy. Indeed, the army and civil service provided invaluable career opportunities for the younger sons of aristocratic families. In practice, the junkers gave up the vestiges of political independence. However, in the area east of the Elbe, where serfdom prevailed, they won absolute social and economic power over the peasantry and the right to exercise justice and local government in their regions. It was only in Cleves–Mark that the nobles by tradition had more limited privileges.

The decline of the Estates left the burgher and peasant classes defenceless and subservient. The urban middle and lower classes were subdued by crushing taxes and the threat of military intervention; the Excise proved a barrier to the economic development of the towns. For instance, in 1662 the authorities of Spandau complained that the burghers had declined to one-fifth of their number prior to the Elector's wars. Compared with Riga or Danzig, Königsberg languished under high tolls and duties after 1674, and the number of ships operating annually from the port was halved to 200 under the Great Elector. But the peasants suffered most, especially as the result of his military campaigns. Many fled west to other states and their lands were left uncultivated. Frederick William's militarization of the state was carried out at a brutal cost to the enserfed peasants of Brandenburg–Prussia.

Cameralism, mercantilism and economic reform

The Great Elector was concerned about the problem of rural depopulation in his lands. He was influenced by the most advanced political and economic ideas of the day, known in Germany as Cameralism. The leaders of the early Cameralist school of political economy in Vienna included Johann-Joachim Becker (1632–82), a chemist and natural philosopher, his son-in-law, William von Hornigk, and the historians, von Seckendorf (1626–92) and Samuel Pufendorf (1632–94). They were concerned with social welfare, administrative efficiency and the state direction of agriculture, industry and trade. In the maritime countries, such as England and the Netherlands, comparable economic ideas were being practised, which came to be known as mercantilism. Western mercantilists also favoured active state intervention to promote their nation's wealth by encouraging the production and export of goods. From his youthful contact with the Netherlands, Frederick William was drawn to the view that a healthy and prosperous people was the basis of a powerful state, and his economic policy reflected the common elements in both these schools of thought.

To stimulate agriculture and counter rural depopulation he turned for help to the Netherlands, inviting Dutch contractors to take over abandoned farms and bring in dairymen and cattle, while involving Dutch technicians in the draining and cultivating of marshland. The Netherlands also provided a stimulus for the development of orchards and gardens. Through the influence of the Electress Louise Henriette, a princess of the House of Orange, a model experimental farm was set up at Oranienburg, north of Berlin, which became a profitable venture. She introduced the cultivation of potatoes, which became a staple diet for the people of Brandenburg. The Elector's thrifty second wife, Dorothea, also set a good example as an estate manager.

The need to encourage self-sufficiency by developing home-based industries was another of the Elector's concerns. In the mercantilist tradition, he favoured trade protection and state monopolies, such as the lucrative monopoly in salt. Wool being one of the country's main natural products, he passed an edict in 1687 to protect the manufacture of woollen cloth and prohibit foreign imports. Similar import prohibitions were imposed on glass, iron, brass, copper, sugar, leather and cheap cloth, in order to foster local production. Simultaneously, the export of raw wool, leather, skins and furs was banned.

Unable to break the restrictive monopoly of the guild system, Frederick William tried instead to entice rural craftsmen to settle in the towns, while immigrants from the Netherlands, France, Piedmont, Switzerland and the Palatinate were lured with inducements such as seed and livestock. Some fifty Jewish families were invited to Brandenburg and promised special protection 'to trade and traffic', provided they kept to strict regulations. The exodus of Huguenots from Louis XIV's France swelled the workforce of Brandenburg by about 20,000. Many of these refugees were professional people – doctors, teachers, architects, soldiers. Others were skilled artisans who found employment in a range of industries: linen, paper, tobacco and the manufacture of silks, hats, wigs, gloves, ribbons, lace, stockings and tapestries. By 1688 a sixth of Brandenburg's population were immigrants. The Great Elector's flexibility and willingness to promote foreigners and commoners of ability, proved a benefit to the state. Among the lawyers of common rank who rose to prominence as councillors and administrators were the Jena brothers and Franz von Meinders. Knyphausen, his Finance Director, came from Friesland; Raule, his Director-General of Marine from Middelburg in the northern Netherlands; Field-Marshal Derfflinger was an Austrian-born commoner. A sixth of the Huguenot immigrants were soldiers, most of whom found service in the Brandenburg army.

Economic development, however, depended not merely on industry and a skilled workforce but also on successful trade, which in turn required good communications. Frederick William was aware of the importance of river systems as natural trade routes. Although Brandenburg controlled a large stretch of the Oder, much trade was being diverted from Silesia to Leipzig in Saxony and thence by the Elbe to Hamburg. To tap into this trade route, a canal was built from the Oder and upper reaches of the Spree, connecting with the Havel, and thence the Elbe (1662–8). By reducing the river tolls on this network, the Great Elector was able to increase the volume of waterborne trade to the advantage of his capital, Berlin. Another innovation was the introduction of a postal service to link the prince's scattered territories, the life-time task of Michael Mathias, Postmaster from 1649 to 1684. Initially intended as an aid to the Electoral administration, the system was opened to citizens and extended to neighbouring commercial centres, such as Danzig, Hamburg and Leipzig. At the same time the Great Elector's interest in overseas trade was stimulated by his naval advisor, Benjamin Raule. To encourage an entrepreneurial spirit, Colleges of Commerce were established in Berlin, Kolberg and Königsberg on Raule's initiative and, copying the example of other maritime states, the Elector launched a chartered company to trade with the Guinea Coast of Africa (1682). A small expedition was sent to found a fortified post, Grossfriedrichsburg, to trade in slaves, gold and ivory. Subsequently Denmark conceded the right to the African Company to establish a slave port on the West Indian island of St Thomas (1685) and the company's European base was transferred from Pillau on the Baltic to the more accessible port of Emden in East Friesland. The venture remained small-scale, however, not least because of the ambivalence of its Dutch competitors.

New-style absolutist, old-style dynast?

How far did the Great Elector succeed in his domestic aims and policies? He was unquestionably a shrewd, strong-willed, dynamic ruler. His successes appear to mark him out as a man of destiny, who steered Brandenburg–Prussia to political and economic recovery after the destruction of the Thirty Years War and set out its future in the four decades from 1648. Convention has it that he created a disciplined standing army, an efficient bureaucracy, uniform institutions and an absolute system of government. As a result he has been credited with laying the foundations of the modern Prussian state (2, p. 253). This interpretation is now being subject to modification (21, p. 185) In most areas, but particularly in the social and economic sphere, there was more retrenchment than innovation in the Great Elector's reign. The nobility continued to enjoy considerable power and privilege. Serfdom was confirmed as the basis of the social structure. In the long term, the Elector's economic policies were insufficient to turn Brandenburg into a commercial or industrial power. On the contrary, the economic development of an urban middle class was retarded, as the economy of Brandenburg–Prussia continued to depend heavily on the land.

Frederick William I was a pragmatist, whose reign was marked by paradox. He was moved by religious motives, concerned for the unity of Protestantism and outraged by Louis XIV's persecution of the Huguenots. Yet he was frequently authoritarian and capable of cynical opportunism and exploitation. He allowed the junker class to become absolute rulers in their own domains, while tying them to the service of the state of Brandenburg–Prussia. When trying to secure financial subsidies from the Estates he argued against their selfish regionalism and in favour of the indivisibility of the state's interests, but he was capable of acting from narrowly personal and dynastic motives. In his testament of 1680 he detailed how his lands and titles were to be distributed between his six surviving sons, ignoring the integrity of state sovereignty. He is said to have had a modern vision of a centralized, unitary state (*Gesamtstaat*), but he was in many ways typical of the Age of Absolutism in remaining at heart a patrimonial prince.

4

The role of Brandenburg–Prussia
in Europe 1688–1740

Elector Frederick III and the Nine Years War 1688–97

The international role of Frederick III was blurred with contra-
diction. As Elector of Brandenburg he was a natural adversary
of an ambitious Emperor. Yet he also believed in the idea of a
universal Christian Empire, and, like his grandfather, George
William, he felt a certain moral commitment to support the
Emperor, so long as this policy coincided with the interests of
Brandenburg–Prussia. As the head of the Calvinist Hohenzollerns, he saw himself as a leader of Protestantism, but in 1688
the principal threat to European peace and stability came not
from the Habsburgs but from another Catholic power, France.
An anti-French policy was already in place when Frederick
succeeded the Great Elector. A series of defensive alliances tied
him to the imperial camp and to the maritime powers of Sweden,
England and the Dutch. Fear of French expansionism kept him
within the anti-French coalition throughout his reign.

The German princes were outraged when in 1688 Louis XIV
exploited his sister-in-law's claim to the Palatinate by sending
his army to occupy the Rhineland electorates of Mainz, Trier,
Cologne and the Palatinate. Frederick was concerned whether
the Empire was militarily prepared. He urged his fellow princes
of Saxony, Hanover and Hesse–Kassel to mobilize under the
banner of the 'Magdeburg Concert'. A combined army of

22,000 men was posted to the central Rhinelands, while the main Brandenburg force protected the Lower Rhine, enabling Frederick's cousin, William of Orange, to lead his invasion of England from the Netherlands. The league's defensive measures were a partial success but they could not prevent the French from devastating Mannheim and Speyer in the Palatinate.

These events opened what came to be known variously as the Nine Years War, the War of the League of Augsburg, or the War of the Palatine Succession. In 1689 the Grand Alliance of Vienna, comprising the Empire, England, the Dutch Republic, Bavaria and Brandenburg–Prussia, was in place: Spain and Savoy were also to join in 1690. The Allies were bent on forcing Louis to give back all the territories he had seized since 1660 and to reaffirm the Peace of Westphalia. When fighting started, Frederick committed his troops to the capture of Kaiserwörth (1689) and the siege of Bonn (1689), which helped to liberate the middle Rhine from the French. Later, Prussian soldiers fought at Steinkerk (1692) and Neerwinden (1693) in the Netherlands. Frederick also sent valuable contingents to help the Emperor on his second front against the Ottoman Turks, and Brandenburg troops were prominent at the battles of Salankemen, Belgrade and Zenta (1691–7).

In the west the Nine Years War soon developed into a war of attrition which inflicted siege and counter-siege on the towns of the Low Countries. By 1692 the more ambitious German princes, including Frederick, had grown sceptical of the value of a conflict from which they stood to make no gains. His father-in-law, Ernest Augustus of Brunswick–Hanover, set about creating a 'third party' of German states that could mediate between France and the Allies. The Emperor intervened to dissuade Duke Ernest Augustus by bribing him with an electoral title. Frederick noted this, hoping it might be a precedent for exploiting Brandenburg's contribution to the war effort. While Ernest Augustus entered on secret negotiations with the Emperor, Frederick was set on persuading Leopold to grant him a royal title. From this time the desire to be recognized as king became Elector Frederick's primary goal and it coloured his relations with the Emperor throughout the 1690s.

In 1697 the Peace of Ryswick brought the grim conflict of the Nine Years War to an end. For some time Frederick had felt aggrieved that the Allies treated him as a mere 'auxiliary' of the

Emperor rather than as a sovereign member of the Grand Alliance. Brandenburg received no territorial gains in the Ryswick settlement, merely the Allies' thanks for his support. If this were not enough, the Elector was additionally vexed when his rival, Augustus II of Saxony, was elected King of Poland (1697). He pressed Leopold to approve his claim to a royal title, but the Emperor was not inclined to make concessions. Habsburg prestige was riding high as French expansionism had been checked. By 1697 Hungary had been reconquered from the Turks and Leopold's son had been elected both King of Hungary and King of the Romans. For Frederick III there was only diplomatic rebuff and humiliation.

International pressures and the royal title 1697–1702

However, the international peace of 1697 was fragile. In the west renewed trouble loomed over the succession to the Spanish Empire; in north-eastern Europe over the dismemberment of the Swedish Empire. Frederick was confident that Brandenburg–Prussia's pivotal position in the east–west axis would enable his state to play a key role. He was prepared to weigh the alternatives of diplomatic neutrality or armed allegiance as a negotiating weapon and means to gain the royal crown. In his own words, 'Seeing that I possess everything that pertains to the dignity of a king . . . why should I not endeavour to achieve the name of king?' (26, p. 56).

In 1699 secret diplomatic discussions started over the royal title between the representatives of Elector Frederick and the Emperor. Leopold was reluctant to create a Protestant monarchy within the Empire, but he had another distraction: the Spanish succession. Charles II of Spain was not expected to live much longer, but the death in 1699 of the Bavarian Electoral prince who was a possible heir to the Spanish Empire reopened the whole succession question. The Emperor was angered by a joint proposal of William III and Louis XIV to partition the Spanish inheritance. Leopold knew that if, as a claimant, he was forced to fight for the Spanish inheritance, Brandenburg–Prussia's military strength would be an asset to his cause. At the same time, the accession of a fifteen-year-old youth, Charles XII, to the Swedish throne in 1697 encouraged Augustus of Saxony–

Poland, Peter I of Russia and Frederick IV of Denmark to plot the seizure of Sweden's Baltic lands. To smooth their path, all three rulers were willing to consider recognizing Frederick's royal title.

The combination of these pressures persuaded Leopold to give way to Frederick's request, although he avoided granting him the royal honour within the Empire. Instead, in 1700 he recognized the Elector's claim to be 'King in Prussia'. Leopold also agreed to use his influence with other powers to secure their recognition of the title. In return, Frederick renewed the 1686 alliance with the Emperor. He promised to supply the imperial armies with 8,000 men if war came and to support Leopold's son and heir, Archduke Joseph, in due course as Holy Roman Emperor. A jubilant Frederick felt he had achieved his main aim; he had vindicated his persistence in negotiation with the Emperor. In an elaborate ceremony at Königsberg in January 1701, he crowned himself and his queen, Sophie Charlotte. It was for him a profound, symbolic act, elevating the prestige of the Hohenzollern dynasty and validating the military statehood of Brandenburg–Prussia in the eyes of his European neighbours.

Two days after the new King Frederick I received imperial recognition of his title, the king of Spain died. The Great Powers failed to achieve a peaceful settlement. Fighting had already started when Frederick joined the princes of the Empire in declaring war on France in 1702.

The War of the Spanish Succession 1702–13

Although the war turned into a world-wide conflict, King Frederick I's concern was with events in Germany. In addition to the protection of his own lands, he saw it as his duty to honour his treaty commitments by supplying troops to the Allies. Prussian forces fought on three fronts. Under Prince Leopold of Anhalt-Dessau they played their part in Marlborough's victory in 1704 at Blenheim in the Danube valley. Another contingent took part, under the imperial commander, Prince Eugene, in the capture of Turin in Italy in 1706, while at Oudenarde and Malplaquet in the Low Countries, the Prussian infantry, watched over by the Crown Prince, made its mark in 1708 and 1709 respectively, in two of the fiercest battles of the war. The new king bathed in the reflected glory of his disciplined fighting machine.

However, the Nine Years War had taught Frederick that he could not rely on the largesse of his allies. He saw the army as a bargaining counter for subsidies to swell his war treasury. He might hope for territorial rewards as well as part of his contribution to the Allied war effort, but he knew that only his military strength would give him political credibility. During the fighting on the Rhine, therefore, he diverted his troops to annex certain counties belonging to the House of Orange: Moers (1702) and Tecklenburg (1707) in the vicinity of Cleves, and Lingen (1702) on the River Ems. He also acquired the principality of Neuchâtel on the borders of Switzerland and Franche–Comté in 1707 when its French ruling family became extinct. At the same time, as heir to the childless William III, who had died in 1702, he did his best to push his dynastic claims to the Orange inheritance. Sometimes, however, he aimed too high and found himself being snubbed. For example, he nursed hopes of being the Allied Supreme Commander but failed to convince the maritime powers (1702). He was also deeply offended when the Emperor later appointed his rival, the Elector of Hanover, to command the armies of the German states.

Although he saw himself as a loyal prince of the Empire, these disappointments caused Frederick to respond from time to time to French diplomatic overtures: thus he acquired a reputation for double-dealing. In 1702 Louis XIV tried to entice him from the Grand Alliance with offers of the cities of Liège and Cologne. In 1704 the Allies feared he might strike a deal with the Elector of Bavaria (who had opted to join the French side), by taking up an offer to occupy Nürnburg and Franconia, the fertile Main basin. Concerned about the effect Prussia's defection would have on the Allied war-power, the Duke of Marlborough twice visited Berlin, in 1704 and 1705, to mollify Frederick with increased subsidies. But as Allied unity began to founder after 1707, the Prussian king felt isolated. There were rancorous exchanges with Hanover, the Dutch and the Emperor over financial arrears, and in self-defence he resumed negotiations with the French in 1709. Diplomatic manoeuvring between Paris and Berlin continued until the peace negotiations at Utrecht in 1712.

Despite an army touching 40,000 men, Frederick's bargaining capacity was weakened by three factors. First, the vulnerability of his western lands, which Marshal Boufflers demonstrated by invading Cleves in 1702; second, his lack of ruthlessness and diplomatic dexterity, which kept him morally bound, yet subordinate to the principal powers of the Grand Alliance; and third, his reluctant involvement in the Baltic conflict. In view of these limitations, he did well to protect his lands from the devastation of war and, on the positive side, to secure his title and achieve territorial gains at the peace. The Treaty of Utrecht, signed shortly after his death in 1713, gave universal recognition to the Prussian king, who was allowed to keep the Orange lands in his possession, together with Upper Guelderland in the Spanish Netherlands as compensation for the part of the Orange inheritance lost to France.

The Great Northern War 1700–21

In spite of Prussia's long-standing designs on Swedish Pomerania, Frederick declined to join the coalition planning to dismember Sweden in 1700. Two years earlier he had been persuaded by Augustus II, the wily ruler of Saxony–Poland, into a rash attack on the Polish–Prussian port of Elbing, after which he was more cautious about committing his army to Baltic adventures. He felt that Brandenburg was not powerful enough to conduct an independent foreign policy on two fronts. The situation in the Baltic was too volatile to be sure of the outcome. Frederick was aware that East Prussia's isolation made it vulnerable, and any attempt to take Polish Prussia or Swedish Pomerania would be strongly resisted by Poland, Russia and Sweden. Charles XII's superhuman defeat of Denmark, Poland and Russia in the years 1700–02 merely convinced him that he had been wise to stand apart from the war with Sweden. In 1703 the Prussian king agreed a treaty with the warrior-king, promising neutrality in return for Swedish recognition of his royal title. A further treaty in 1707 provided mutual territorial guarantees between Sweden and Prussia. But for the most part, in his capacity as King in Prussia, Frederick adhered to the principle of armed neutrality, while as ruler of Brandenburg he supported the maritime powers and the Emperors Leopold (1658–1705) and Joseph (1705–11) against France. After 1704 he had the added security of knowing that the Allies were willing to guarantee the integrity of his lands.

Nevertheless, he could still be tempted occasionally by chimerical schemes with prospects of acquiring more land. For example, the Tsar's agent, Patkul, a Lithuanian nobleman deeply hostile to Charles XII, tried in 1704 to inveigle Frederick into providing troops for a joint Russo–Polish–Prussian attack on Sweden. Frederick had already toyed the year before with a Russian plan to partition Sweden's possessions and allocate to him those parts of Pomerania and Prussia his family had coveted for years. Now, a clumsy attempt by Frederick to intervene in Danzig (1704) backfired, annoying his maritime allies, who were sensitive to any change in the northern balance of power. Nor did they approve of Frederick's over-optimistic attempts to restore peace by acting as mediator between Russia and Sweden: initiatives which came to nothing since neither power would compromise.

After 1709 the balance of power in north-eastern Europe shifted noticeably. In that year, the Swedish army was crushed by the Russians at Poltava in the Ukraine. In 1714 it was the turn of the Swedish fleet at Hango. Charles XII himself fled to Turkey. The collapse of his empire then threatened to embroil the whole of Europe in one great war. Caught in the middle, Frederick began to question the wisdom of neutrality. Earlier, he had tried somewhat ingenuously to negotiate a partition of Poland with Sweden's arch-enemies, Peter I and Augustus II, without committing himself to an offensive alliance against the Swedes. However, the Tsar insisted that Prussia should declare war on Sweden. Frederick procrastinated for too long, and in 1709 Swedish troops defiantly marched through Prussian territory. Although the western Allies tried to contain hostilities in the Baltic by treating as neutral Sweden's German lands (Neutrality Conventions of The Hague, 1710) they could not prevent the passage of Russian, Polish and Saxon troops across Brandenburg–Prussia to Swedish Pomerania in 1711. The Prussian king's last throw of the diplomatic dice, a proposal for a Prusso–Swedish–Saxon alliance against Russia (1712), was finally sabotaged by the Swedish king. The Great Northern War outlasted Frederick. On balance he had neither gained nor lost by remaining largely passive.

His successor, King Frederick William I, was also cautious of military involvement, but he enjoyed certain advantages. With the ending of the Spanish Succession War his battle-hardened troops were freed for service elsewhere. In the continuing absence of Charles XII, the Swedish government was more conciliatory. As an unknown quantity the new Prussian king was at first treated circumspectly by both Sweden and Russia. Sweden put up no resistance to the seizure of Stettin by a Prussian force in 1713, a concession Frederick William took to be a preliminary to permanent occupation. It had already spurred him to sign a treaty in 1714, agreeing to a secret partition of Sweden's Baltic states with the Russian Tsar, when the dramatic return of Charles XII from Turkey reactivated the war and forced Frederick William to side openly with the anti-Swedish coalition.

Circumstances had propelled Frederick William into abandoning neutrality. Besides wishing to conciliate Peter I, he was keen to cut as conspicuous a figure as his cousin, Elector George of Hanover, who became King of Great Britain in 1714 and who had also joined the anti-Swedish coalition. In 1714 the two kings agreed to support each other's claims: Frederick William's to Stettin and the southern half of Swedish Pomerania; George's to Bremen and Verden. To show that he was in earnest, Frederick William sent Prussian troops to join the Saxon-Danish forces closing in on Wismar and Stralsund in 1715. But the appearance of the Russian army in Mecklenburg the following year alarmed Frederick William. The Allies could not agree on an invasion of Sweden, and after Charles XII's mysterious death in 1718, the Prussian king detached himself from Russia with British persuasion, and followed Hanover into making peace with Sweden. By the Treaty of Stockholm in 1720 Frederick William agreed to pay 2,000,000 thalers for Western Pomerania as far as the River Peene, including the prized port of Stettin and the islands of Usedom and Wollin. Despite failing in his bid for the whole province, his reputation was much enhanced by his gaining what the Great Elector had tried but failed to win.

In time the consequences of the Northern War became clear. Sweden, like Poland, was in irretrievable decline. But basking in success, and reluctant to antagonize the Tsar, Frederick William refused to intervene to moderate the final Russo-Swedish peace settlement at Nystad in 1721. As a result, Peter the Great wrested the Baltic states of Livonia, Estonia, Ingria and Karelia from Sweden. The Prussian king also agreed that Peter, already the guarantor of the Swedish constitution, should have similar rights over Poland–Lithuania (1720). He was tacitly admitting the daunting presence of an ambitious new Russian empire on the Baltic.

Frederick William I and collective security in the west 1720–40

The Peace of Utrecht had established limits to French expansion and had given substantial territorial compensation to the Austrian Habsburgs, taking them to the zenith of their power. In a series of mutual guarantees, such as the Quadruple Alliance of 1718, the great powers tried to provide a system of collective security which would ensure peace for the next generation. Frederick William had himself signed the treaty of Amsterdam with France and Russia in 1717 in support of the Utrecht settlement and aiming to enlist French mediation in the Northern War. Such treaties did not prevent alliances from shifting nor intermittent crises from developing, as countries jockeyed to protect their interests.

From Prussia's perspective the new balance had in-built limitations. One was the preponderance of the Habsburg Empire, which stretched from Hungary to Milan and from the Netherlands to Sardinia (exchanged for Sicily in 1718). Another was the influence of Hanover, now linked with the naval and commercial power of Great Britain. The rivalry between the two German kings almost brought Frederick William to attack Hanover in 1729. Third, there was a question mark over Russia's ambitions to expand westwards. And a final concern arose from the tendency of the great powers after 1713 to sacrifice the interests of smaller powers in their efforts to maintain the peace. Brandenburg had certain territorial ambitions. By gaining West Prussia, which stood between the electorate and royal East Prussia, the Prussian kingdom would be united into the largest German state. Frederick William remained constantly vigilant.

Hereditary claims and succession issues dominated international relations in the years 1720 to 1740. Since the ailing Elector Carl Philip, ruler of Jülich–Berg, had no sons, Frederick William decided to revive his family rights to the duchies, to which Emperor Charles VI also had a claim. Charles, meanwhile, was determined to protect his daughter's succession to the Habsburg inheritance, according to the terms of a special legal arrangement known as the Pragmatic Sanction. When the king of Spain signed the Treaty of Vienna with the Emperor in 1725, promising to recognize the Austrian succession, the British and French responded with the counter-alliance of Hanover. To avoid being isolated, Frederick William quickly became a signatory too, by the Herrenhausen Convention (1725). However, when Russia and Saxony moved into the Austrian camp in 1726, he was even more alarmed. An agreement between the two largest land empires was a threat to Prussia. He abandoned the Hanover alliance in favour of a rapprochement with Austria and Russia, sealed by the Treaty of Westerhausen. Two years later, in 1728, the Treaty of Berlin confirmed the Austro-Prussian alliance. In exchange for Prussia's guarantee of the Pragmatic Sanction, Charles VI promised moral support for the Hohenzollern claim to a share of Jülich–Berg. But by 1731 Austro-Prussian relations had cooled, as Frederick William realized he could not rely on the Emperor's support over Jülich–Berg. Nor could he count on his ally to settle Prussia's rumbling friction with Hanover. But Frederick William did not feel confident enough of his position to break with the Emperor, and his apprehension grew when, in 1731, George II signed a treaty of mutual guarantee with Charles VI that provided security for Hanover.

Attention soon focused on another disputed succession, in Poland. Frederick William hoped that by supporting the Austrian candidate, Augustus of Saxony, he might ingratiate himself with the Emperor and coax the Poles into ceding some territory. All the same, he allowed the French claimant to the Polish crown, Stanislas Leszczynski, to cross Prussian soil *en route* to Poland. France then seized the opportunity to attack the Habsburgs in Italy and the lower Rhine. As a sovereign king who had signed the Pragmatic Sanction, Frederick William honourably offered his army to the Emperor, whose pride only allowed him to accept an electoral contingent. But the War of the Polish Succession from 1733 to 1735 went badly for the Austrians, as did the Austro-Turkish War of 1736–9. This time Frederick William refused the use of his troops, offering the Emperor a gift of 1.2 million thalers instead, in return for guaranteeing the Hohenzollern succession to Berg. However, the Prussian king found there was no glory or gratitude in siding with the Austrian Empire, and he remained wary of the Russians. In fact, he found himself friendless when Austria, France, Britain and the Netherlands came together to support the rival Palatinate line in Jülich–Berg. Furious at what appeared to be another Great Power conspiracy and act of imperial treachery, Frederick William turned to Prussia's old enemy, France. The astute French minister, Cardinal Fleury, exploited the Austro-Prussian rift. He guaranteed part of the Jülich–Berg inheritance to Prussia in a secret treaty concluded in 1739. But ironically the ruler of Jülich–Berg, Carl Philip (1716–42), was to outlive Frederick William by two years.

Towards Great Power status?

King Frederick I has had a bad press. He ruled at a time when Brandenburg–Prussia was forced to look in two directions, to the west, which was still the geo-political hub of Europe, and to the eastern nexus, which was growing in prominence. Except for the years 1699–1701, his reign was spent in wars which he did not cause; nor had he the power and ability to influence their outcome. He was easily dwarfed by contemporary monarchs, Louis XIV, Charles XII, Peter the Great and Emperor Leopold I. So it is easy to echo Droysen's jibe that he pursued 'in the West war without politics, in the East politics without war' (26, p. 4). Frederick is also accused of having wasted money and men on the vainglorious pursuit of his royal title. The criticism takes no account of the prime importance attached to symbols of authority and status in this age. In 1732, when Frederick William added the emblem of the county of East Friesland to his coat of arms, he was making a similar, though less elevated, statement.

Whereas the period 1688–1720 was an age of international conflict, 1720–40 was a period of relative harmony, and this worked to Frederick William's advantage. During his reign the centre of political gravity began to shift from the west to the east-centre of Europe. The decline of Sweden, Poland and Turkey gave Russia, Austria and Prussia an opportunity to extend their spheres of influence or round off their territories. But the impressive phase of Prussian expansion was to occur after 1740, and Frederick William's claim that the power of the sword surpassed that of the pen was mere rhetoric. His foreign policy was cautious and conservative: peaceful, not expansionist. It was a paradox in a king who possessed such an impressive army that he treated it as a deterrent, rather than a tool of war.

Neither Frederick I nor Frederick William I was at home in the subtle world of diplomacy. Both rulers were committed in principle to the Empire and to alliance with the Habsburg Emperor, although both also indulged in intrigues with imperial enemies when political necessity demanded. As a result they aroused widespread mistrust. Father and son shared a belief that political authority came from military superiority. They each contributed to the Hohenzollern imperative to enlarge their possessions. If the Great Elector laid the foundations of Prussian policy and created a place for Brandenburg in Europe's diplomatic network, Frederick I and Frederick William I further consolidated the standing of the Prussian state, bequeathing a permanent European role to the Crown Prince, who succeeded as King Frederick II in May 1740.

5

The domestic policies of the first two kings 1700–40

In domestic matters, as well as foreign policy, historians have been unwilling to give much credit to the Elector-King Frederick. His policies have been dismissed as wasteful or unproductive, in sharp contrast to those of his successor, King Frederick William. The denigration of Frederick's reputation began with his grandson, Frederick the Great. Even one of his biographers admits: 'Dwarfed by the achievements and reputations of his father and of his son, Frederick . . . has also been dwarfed in the historical memory' (**26**, p. 1). This was partly a matter of personality. Frederick lacked the spartan toughness and resolve of the other two kings. He had certain tastes that were atypical of the Hohenzollerns, such as a love of precious jewels. As a well-meaning paternalist he wanted to win his people's affection by lightening their burdens. It was a very different attitude from his son's. Frederick William never hid his contempt for individuals or for whole groups of his subjects. From this it was logical to assume that the policies of the two rulers were quite different.

Like most princes of his day, Frederick admired and modelled himself on Louis XIV of France, who was his godfather, although they were at war with one another for most of his reign. French was the language of his court, where French fashion and ceremonial also prevailed. Frederick regarded these external trappings, including the royal title, which, as we have seen, he pursued assiduously by diplomatic means, as important political symbols. In fact, in this respect Frederick was merely perpetuating an existing trend. Already under the Great Elector French influences were superseding Dutch; luxurious and ostentatious living replaced his once frugal lifestyle, and Versailles inspired his new residences at Potsdam, Copenick and Orianenburg. But it was Frederick's admiration for French culture and his slavish imitation of the Sun King (even to ordering an exact copy of Louis XIV's wig for himself) which divided him completely from King Frederick William. While Frederick believed the key to successful absolutism lay in the public display of wealth and pomp, his son believed that power came from the rigorous management of the state's limited resources. In addition, by 1713 the European scene was changing: the age of Louis XIV was past. The new Prussian king despised the foppishness of French courtly manners and hated extravagance of any sort. Parsimonious by nature, he became obsessed with cleanliness, short hair and the simple, austere lifestyle of a German soldier. And yet, despite their differing role models, there was a fair degree of continuity in the domestic running of Brandenburg–Prussia in the period 1700–40.

The development of a military state

In the case of the army, continuity was provided by the commitment of the Hohenzollern kings to establish Brandenburg–Prussia as a strong military power through the presence of a standing army. It was also helped by loyal commanders like Prince Leopold of Anhalt–Dessau, who served three of those rulers with distinction (1693–1747). The first, the Elector-King Frederick, gave the army a strong sense of identity. From 1701 the various contingents were known as 'the Prussian army', identified by uniforms based on the colours of the king's coat of arms: red, blue and black. Frederick William went further. From 1725 he took to wearing military uniform at court as a matter of routine – as did his courtiers – a custom which foreign visitors found bizarre at first, but one which symbolized the army's overriding significance. It is no wonder that he was dubbed the 'royal drill sergeant'.

Frederick, moreover, not only maintained the Great Elector's army and took over its leadership personally, but increased its manpower by one third to about 40,000 men by 1713, doubling the number of grenadiers, the 'shock troops' of the infantry. He established a central armoury in Berlin (1700) and with the encouragement of the scientist, Leibniz, continued the modernization started by his father, approving the use of the flintlock musket and socket bayonet to replace the matchlock and pike. As firepower and the value of disciplined infantry formations overshadowed the role of the cavalry, the latter were reduced in numbers. Frederick William was totally dedicated to his guardsmen and encouraged unorthodox methods to conscript men of exceptional height to the guards, from foreign states as well as his own territories. Under him the number of soldiers rose dramatically to 80,000 by the time of his death in 1740.

Both rulers, therefore, considered the army to be of the utmost importance and made all the final decisions on military matters, although in Frederick's case only after consultation with his officers and ministers in the War Council. It was his decision to take power from the regimental colonels and to insist that officers were to be promoted, disciplined and dismissed on the king's order. Furthermore, promotion was to be by merit, not simply by custom or seniority (1695). It was a change which proved difficult to enforce on officers of noble birth and one that King Frederick William decided to reverse. Both rulers, however, tried to safeguard the quality of the officer class. Under Frederick middle-class recruits were still able to become officers, but under Frederick William the officer corps became the exclusive domain of the nobility. Frederick established cadet academies for young officers in Berlin (1701) and Kolberg (1703). Both he and his successor forbade the nobility to serve in foreign armies. In 1722 Frederick William urged nobles to compel their sons to join a cadet training school but he also took the precaution of ordering the provincial councillor, or *Landrat*, to forward a list of junkers' sons to be registered for military service in a Table of Vassals. The king combined his father's two military academies and set up another at Magdeburg (1719).

All these measures reflected a major problem facing the Prussian kings: the question of recruitment. Draconian discipline did not eliminate the problem of desertion, and the practice remained of recruiting foreigners. But in 1693 Frederick issued a Recruiting Edict, forcing every province to provide a stipulated number of recruits, and in 1708 he instituted per capita fines if they failed to produce their quota of soldiers. In 1714 Frederick William decreed that the peasantry had a lifelong obligation to do military service. He also returned to the principle of regional conscription in his important Recruitment Edict of 1733. This introduced a cantonal system in which the registration of soldiers was to take place within defined districts or cantons of 5,000 households. By 1740 one in twenty-five subjects was serving in the Prussian army.

In the course of forty years (1700–40) the two kings adopted some different policies, as might be expected. In 1701 Frederick borrowed the Great Elector's strategy of raising a Land Militia to serve for five years and defend the frontiers and fortresses of the territories. By 1703 some 20,000 men aged between eighteen and forty years were under arms as militiamen. Frederick William, however, discontinued this system, believing that it was both inefficient and undermined recruitment to the standing army. As we have seen, Frederick and his son also diverged on the social composition of the officer corps. Frederick William oversaw the creation of a caste of noble officers as a means of creating social cohesion. Indeed, military needs came to dictate the social structure of the country. By 1740 a rigid system was in place, by which the nobility was identified with the officer class and the exploited peasantry with the military rank-and-file. This necessitated a careful balancing act. A series of royal decrees (1709, 1714, 1739, 1749) sought to protect the peasants from excessive service demands from their lords to ensure smooth recruitment of the peasants to the army. Frederick William's early interest in military matters became an obsession. Generals took precedence over royal ministers at court. He enjoyed the details of military administration, supervising military drill and ensuring that off-duty soldiers worked as wool or cotton spinners. In an unusual display of paternalism, he urged his son not to reduce his soldiers' pay. He raised the expenditure on the army from 50 per cent, as it was under King Frederick, to a phenomenal 80 per cent of the national revenue. By 1740 the army did not exist to serve the country; Brandenburg–Prussia was a country existing for its army. This was an extraordinary state of affairs, which was bound to have considerable political and economic consequences.

Financial and economic matters

King Frederick I is rarely credited with financial success, although his biographers have defended the achievements of his reign. The Finance Director, von Knyphausen, carried forward the reforms started under the Great Elector. In 1689 the Controller's office (*Hofkammer*), a central accounting bureau, was finally established, and with it a general budget for the state. Knyphausen also ensured that revenue went to the appropriate treasury, for it was not until 1711 that a general treasury was set up. With the support of Frederick's leading minister, Eberhard Christoph Danckelmann, revenues were increased from a number of sources: the postal system, poll tax, luxury taxes (on wigs and carriages, for example) and the extension of monopolies. However, these proved insufficient to meet government needs in time of war, and by 1697 the finances were in severe deficit. The king blamed his ministers for mismanagement, yet the political downfall of Danckelmann and Knyphausen brought no improvement. The rise of a new royal favourite, Count von Wartenberg, during the years 1697–1711, coincided with a downturn in the country's financial affairs.

The doubling of the expenses of the court and government was one factor in this deterioration. The extravagant coronation of King Frederick and his queen in 1701 cost six million thalers, which had to be raised by a special tax. The ceremony in Königsberg, which resembled the imperial coronation, was designed to impress not only the king's subjects but the rest of Europe. In addition to the cost of the army, new royal buildings and a severe outbreak of plague in Prussia between 1708 and 1713 placed strains on the treasury. Frederick was too lethargic to control the greed and corruption of Wartenberg and his circle. Frederick William later claimed that the state finances were on the brink of bankruptcy at his accession, and one of his first aims was to overhaul them. Unlike his father, he refused to borrow money from Jewish merchants or wealthy nobles. Instead, he set out to create a strong reserve, embarking first on the reform of the way the crown lands were administered by placing them under a general Finance Directory. In the course of his reign revenues from the crown lands almost trebled to 3.3

million thalers. He also found new ways of increasing taxation. The number of goods subject to excise increased to include not only imported luxuries but domestic goods such as dairy produce. Twice, in 1714 and 1721, he dealt firmly with the Estates of Cleves and Mark after confirming the Recess of 1660–61 agreed by his grandfather. Prussian soldiers were duly ordered in to impose the Excise in addition to the traditional *Contribution* voted by the Estates. However, Frederick William was not satisfied until he had taxed the nobility. In 1715 Prussian junkers were subjected to a land tax; elsewhere the nobles paid a levy in lieu of feudal services.

In his modest way King Frederick had tried to sustain the Great Elector's economic policy. He supported the African Company and the postal service. New postal routes were opened linking Berlin with Vienna (1692) and with Cleves and the Netherlands (1694), while new offices appeared in Pomerania (1698) and Mecklenburg (1712). Operations were regularized in the Postal Ordinance of 1712. Commerce was helped by a fixed rate of exchange, the setting up of a rudimentary board of trade, the encouragement given to enterprising immigrants and the supervision of the guilds which represented backward-looking vested interests. To stimulate farming Frederick also approved a new system of heritable leasehold tenure on Crown lands, but it had to be abandoned after grain prices fell (1710). His successor deplored the system and after his accession redeemed the leases. Frederick William regarded a well-populated land and flourishing rural economy based on leasehold tenure as the key to prosperity, hence his measures to encourage the resettlement of plague-stricken Prussia (1716–18). He had no interest in colonial ventures. 'I have always regarded this trading nonsense as a chimera', he said dismissively of the African Company before selling it off to the Dutch at a knock-down price in 1721. As a Cameralist, he favoured state protection for manufacturing industries, such as woollen cloth, leather and iron, which were essential for the army, but his main concern was the scrupulous collection and accounting of taxation in all its forms to increase income and produce a treasury surplus. As a result, in 1740 he left Brandenburg–Prussia with an annual revenue of seven million thalers, compared with four million in 1713.

Government and bureaucracy

Continuity between the Great Elector's government and Elector-King Frederick's reign was provided by a group of able ministers and courtiers who remained in office for many years: men like Fuchs, Meinders, Grumbkow, Knyphausen, Danckelmann, and the Kraut brothers, who between them ran most branches of the administration. Others continued to serve into the next reign: von Printzen was in charge of religion, education and the household, and von Ilgen helped to direct foreign affairs for thirty-three years.

The first decade of Frederick's reign was the high point of the Privy Council's existence, but it had already ceased to be a decision-making body and become an administrative one. However, after his purge of ministers (1697) Frederick resorted to an inner set of advisers or councillors as the Great Elector had done in his last years. Frederick wanted to take personal direction of the government and to improve the judicial system. In 1703 he secured the right to be the last source of appeal for all his lands and a supreme court of appeal was duly set up at Kölln. An ordinance of 1709 began the reform of procedure, but it was too soon to hope for judicial uniformity. There were still separate superior courts in the provinces and the various religious sects were allowed their own tribunals. Sometimes Frederick intervened personally in local matters and, surprisingly, in aspects of daily life such as Sunday observance and burial regulations; he also tried to control gambling, card games and immorality. But in general he lacked the drive and energy to run the country. Instead, he relied on a small caucus led by Wartenberg who met with him in his chamber. This arrangement has been referred to as a form of cabinet government, though in reality it was absolute government by favourites. However, to ensure that his policies were carried out in the regions, Frederick appointed a number of judicial officials as royal agents, known as fiscals. Their authority quickly developed and they became invaluable to the central government as the ears and eyes of the king.

Frederick William served his apprenticeship in government towards the end of his father's reign. With Wartenberg in disgrace, Frederick came to rely on his son. Frederick William was a shrewd administrator. He was also as intelligent and cunning as he was uncouth. He set out to achieve two goals: effective centralization through the bureaucracy and absolute personal government. He abolished Privy Council meetings with ministers and made all final decisions himself, developing an effective and loyal civil service to implement his policies. In 1723 he carried through his major reform, the merging of the old General War Commissariat and the General Finance Directory into a single institution, the General Directory, or to give its full name, the *General-Ober-Finanz-Kriegs-und-Domanen-Direktorium*. The new body, which was under his personal presidency, directed the whole financial administration at both provincial and central level. It had four departments, meeting once a week, each with a minister and a number of councillors who dealt with specific geographical regions and general functions, such as the supply and billeting of troops. To complete the state administration, the Foreign Office was reorganized in 1728. There was also a separate Department of Justice and Ecclesiastical Affairs. Frederick William expected the highest standards of service from his officials. He used a combination of 'sticks' and 'carrots' to instil the principle of service to the state, demanding efficiency and total obedience. Retired or disabled soldiers were encouraged to man the bureaucracy. The king also had a preference for Prussians, whom he regarded as 'very intelligent', but to be on the safe side a network of fiscals, official spies and informants operated throughout the provinces. Meanwhile the king set an example by working indefatigably; he saw himself as the first servant of the state: 'I am the finance minister and field marshal of the King of Prussia', he proclaimed. In an age when venality was commonplace in Europe, he created an exceptional administrative machine. It is for this reason that he has been called 'the father of Prussian bureaucracy' and 'the greatest domestic king' in the state's history (**10**, II, pp. 192, 196).

Styles of royal absolutism

The style and image of the monarchy was somewhat different under the first two Prussian kings. By winning the title of king, Frederick raised his political reputation and the status of Brandenburg–Prussia. He supported the conventional view that a lavish court was a symbol of power and prestige. Frederick William, on the other hand, scorned palaces and civil ceremonies, though he loved military pomp. He lived above the major state offices and turned the gardens into a drill ground. He regarded the army, not the court, as the main instrument of political strength and authority.

However, both kings built on the Great Elector's traditions, in enlarging and strengthening the standing army, harnessing the nobility to military service and directing the administration of the country from the centre so that the old corporate groups, such as the Estates and the guilds, ceased to have a serious function. Both rulers were interventionists. Frederick's various reforms helped to raise living standards, but Frederick William saw his main achievement as leaving a formidable army and full treasury. While the Great Elector still regarded his lands as personal possessions, there was a sea-change after Frederick established the Prussian kingdom in 1701. The state had a coherent identity, which Frederick William endorsed on his accession. In an important edict of 1713 he declared that all Hohenzollern territories constituted an indivisible whole and the crown lands were an inalienable trust. The process of welding these lands into an organic union (*Gesamtstaat*) occurred during the years 1700–40. At the same time royal absolutism was also established. Frederick believed in a hierarchical system. He thought of himself as the father of his people, but he was a fatalist, open to influence by stronger characters. His absolutism was therefore exercised haphazardly and not always wisely. Frederick William, on the other hand, was an authentic despot. As he warned the nobles, 'I shall establish my sovereignty like a rock of bronze' (**10**, II, p. 202).

6
Social and cultural developments
1648–1740

The social and cultural climate of Brandenburg–Prussia is usually portrayed as harsh, coarse and philistine. North German society was imbued with a sense of inferiority as contemporaries drew unfavourable comparisons with France and Italy, but even neighbouring Protestant states like Saxony and the courts of Brunswick and Hanover surpassed Brandenburg as centres of cultural patronage and learning. To the cultivated Austrian rulers the Great Elector had the reputation of a 'vandal of the north'. His successor, the melancholy Elector-King Frederick, was ridiculed in the European courts for being an 'ape of Louis XIV', while King Frederick William I was an irascible boor with no cultural sensitivity.

This unflattering picture of the Hohenzollerns contains a good deal of truth. In the early modern period the 'high culture' of brilliant minds and great artists contrasted with brutal social and judicial standards which nowadays would amount to the very antithesis of a 'cultured' society. Peasants and common soldiers were subjected to exploitation and ferocious discipline. Even Frederick I decreed that deserters should have their nose and one ear cut off before serving hard labour for life (1711). An unforgiving ethos applied to the highest and the lowest in the land. When Crown Prince Frederick plotted to flee the country, his father, King Frederick William I, ordered him to watch the execution of his accomplice and friend, Lieutenant

Katte. For all that, the Hohenzollerns were pious Calvinists. They were brought up in the stern tradition of the Reformed Church which put duty above mere social and cultural considerations and frowned on sensuality and worldliness. (The lavish royal coronation of 1701 could be justified on political grounds.) The Hohenzollerns openly expressed their solemn piety. In the words of the Great Elector, 'our faith and our consciences imposes on us a duty . . . we are accountable to God'. His words were echoed by his son and grandson. 'I will submit my will entirely to God's', King Frederick assured his wife, while King Frederick William boasted in his political testament, 'I have always laboured . . . to live a godly life.' And yet, despite the sober and sometimes pedestrian atmosphere of the Hohenzollern court, some members of the dynasty had cultural pretensions and they ensured that Brandenburg–Prussia was associated with some of Europe's leading intellectuals and artists.

Religious toleration

In spite of their adherence to a puritanical creed, by the standards of the day the Hohenzollerns were remarkably tolerant of different religious sects. The Great Elector regarded Lutheranism and the Reformed faith of Calvinism as entirely compatible. His open-door policy towards the Huguenots and the Jews has been mentioned already. Although economic factors coloured his religious ecumenism – this was also true of Elector-King Frederick – the terms of the Potsdam Decree of 1685, offering the French Huguenots 'safe and free asylum', illustrated a pragmatic nature, and even an enlightened attitude. A number of French intellectuals were among the Huguenot immigrants, and one of them, Jacques de Gaultier, became the Great Elector's personal physician. Encouraged by his court preacher, Jablonski, Frederick maintained his father's all-embracing policy, so much so that his reign has been called the golden age of the refugee. His queen, Sophie Charlotte, set an example by choosing a Huguenot as her personal chaplain. During Frederick's reign, the Huguenots were given their own courts, code of law, churches, colleges, hospitals and bank; and his Naturalization Edict (1709) gave them equal opportunities with local Germans to obtain a range of positions. He also offered sanctuary to other Protestants from states as far apart as Hungary and the Palatinate. It was Frederick's wish to see a union of the evangelical Protestants, a moderate, all-embracing church on the model of the Anglican Church.

Under the Hohenzollerns the clergy became in effect state servants, and the rulers enjoyed a beneficent absolute power over the church as well as the state. There was some hostility between the Lutheran majority and the members of the Calvinist, Reformed Church, but the lack of religious bigotry on the part of the Great Elector and his successors and the people's acceptance of their paternalism obviated any serious religious strife. In fact, the inculcation of Christian values was an integral part of the reform of popular culture which took place under the Hohenzollerns; as the historian Michael Hughes observed, 'Toleration produced intellectual freedom and an openness in Brandenburg–Prussia not seen in most other German states' (**11**, p. 143).

This tolerance was shown not merely to the two main branches of Protestantism but under Frederick, albeit somewhat grudgingly, to his Catholic subjects, most of whom lived in the cities of Halle, Halberstadt, Magdeburg and Berlin. He also accepted a limited number of Jewish families, who paid 3,000 thalers a year to the state in return for letters of protection and guarantees of freedom of worship. Even heretics, mystics and rationalists were not turned away but found refuge in Frederick's Berlin, although his son was more rigid. In 1723 King Frederick William expelled the rationalist philosopher, Christian von Wolff, from his university post for alleged subversion.

Another group to benefit under both Frederick and his successor were the Pietists, whose community was an offshoot of the Lutheran Church. Pietism was a reaction against institutionalized religion. It promoted a universalist outlook but also practical good works and the spiritual awakening of the individual. Driven out of Saxony, the first leader of the Pietists in Germany, Philipp Jacob Spener (1635–1705), took refuge in Berlin in 1691. With the tacit approval of the Elector Frederick and his minister Fuchs, Spener and his followers, August Hermann Francke (1663–1727), a theologian and orientalist, and the distinguished philosopher Christian Thomasius (1655–1728), established Pietism in the new university of Halle.

Thomasius broke new ground by lecturing in German rather than Latin. In addition, by separating philosophy from theology he was to make Halle the leading centre for new cultural thought in Protestant Germany. Meanwhile, in 1695 the Francke Institute was founded; this included a school for the poor, an orphanage, a medical dispensary and a publishing house. Although Frederick later withdrew his support from the movement, blaming the Pietists for the mental illness of his wife, Francke won the favour of the new king, Frederick William I, in 1713. Having visited the Pietist orphanage in Halle in 1711, he applauded the puritanical discipline of the regime there and from that time he gave his patronage and protection to Francke's activities.

The Pietists drew attention to the value of popular education. They encouraged both kings, Frederick and Frederick William, to promote religious education. But the Great Elector had already shown an interest in educational matters: in appointing Otto von Schwerin as tutor to his sons, he had chosen a highly intelligent, scholarly and principled man. The elector took steps to provide *gymnasia* or humanistic schools in the provinces and he set up a university at Duisburg, to complement those at Frankfurt and Königsberg and serve the people of his Rhenish lands. In 1661 he opened his personal library of over 20,000 books and manuscripts and his collection of medals and antiquities to the public, and later he began the building of a state library, housed in the royal castle, which was completed under Frederick. The Great Elector's last service to learning was to persuade the great jurist and historian, Samuel Pufendorf (1632–94), to leave Sweden and settle in Berlin.

However, it was the Elector-King Frederick who appointed Pufendorf to be royal historian and commissioned him to write the history of his father's and his own reign. Frederick can be credited with a number of educational initiatives. In 1706 he ordered the setting up of schools in every Pomeranian village; in 1708 a Royal Commission was set up to revise textbooks; and an edict of 1710 ordered inspectors to find out how many teachers there were in Brandenburg. Under him secondary schools were founded in Halle and Berlin, and the Latin schools in the capital and in Königsberg flourished. New schools were founded for both artisans and nobles, the latter to instil such gentlemanly arts as riding, fencing and dancing. Frederick also gave financial support to private schools, such as the Fredericianum, which under its Pietist director pioneered the importance of understanding rather than rote learning and had considerable influence on German education. The king's most notable achievement, however, was to establish in 1694 a new university at Halle to produce administrators for government service. Encouraged by the Pietists and by his ministers, Fuchs and Danckelmann, Frederick succeeded in attracting a number of leading scholars there, the most eminent being the philosopher, Christian Wolff (1679–1754). On Leibniz's recommendation he was appointed Professor of Mathematics in 1707, a position he held for sixteen years. Wolff was known as an exponent of Rationalism and he became a leading figure in the German Enlightenment.

Frederick William was also concerned with the need to educate efficient administrators. In 1729 he founded chairs of Economics at the universities of Halle and Frankfurt to promote the fashionable theory of Cameralism. In the Pietist tradition he established schools and orphanages, but an edict of 1717, ordering parents to send their children to school, could not be enforced. In all, it was Frederick I who was most persuaded of the importance of education, art and learning as means of enhancing the state and of adding to the glory of the Hohenzollern dynasty.

Scholarship, science, the arts and the state

In the seventeenth and early eighteenth centuries there was a rapid evolution of knowledge that has been called the Scientific Revolution. This momentous movement produced both a revolution in mathematics and natural philosophy known as 'the new sciences', and a fusion of pure and applied science from which came important technological progress. One of the experimental scientists who helped to advance technology was the physicist and natural philosopher, Otto von Guericke (1602–86). A native of Magdeburg and for thirty-five years mayor of that city, which had been ceded to Brandenburg–Prussia by the Peace of Westphalia, he was befriended by the Great Elector. Guericke produced the first air pump in 1650, using it to study the qualities of vacuum and the role of air in combustion and respiration. He dedicated his treatise on the notion of vacuum to Elector Frederick William. Guericke also invented a proto-type of an electric generator (1663) with which he produced static electricity. This empirical approach to science was comp-lemented in the next half-century by the work of polymaths like Gottfried Leibniz (1646–1716), who was part of a great European mathematical tradition that included Galileo, Boyle, Descartes, Huygens and Newton. The genius of Leibniz influ-enced every branch of knowledge from logic to jurisprudence, mechanics to theology and history, and made him a seminal figure in the evolution of a systematic theory of knowledge.

A Saxon by birth, Leibniz settled in Hanover (1676) and was befriended by the ruling family, including Sophie Charlotte before she became Electress of Brandenburg. Through Sophie Charlotte's influence, Elector Frederick III invited Leibniz to Berlin in 1697 and was persuaded by Leibniz to follow the example of such states as France and England and found a state academy of learning which would enhance the international reputation of Brandenburg–Prussia. Hence, in 1700, the Society of Sciences (later renamed the Academy of Sciences) was estab-lished with Leibniz as its first Director. He remained a regular visitor to Brandenburg until 1711, stayed a close confidant of Sophie Charlotte until her death in 1705 and finally dedicated one of his works, *Theodicy* (1710), to the late Queen.

King Frederick had learned from the Great Elector the politi-cal value of attracting eminent or gifted Europeans to his court. It must be admitted that compared with Leibniz or Pufendorf, many of those invited to Berlin were men of second rank. Frederick was himself neither a scholar nor a great connoisseur. He appreciated music a little more than his father, having been required to learn the flute and clavichord as a boy. But it is said that the only secular music heard in Berlin was the sound of the trumpets and drums of military bands: an unfortunate contrast to the rich musical tradition of Protestant Germany at this time. On the other hand, Sophie Charlotte had been brought up to enjoy music. She delighted in the fashionable Italian operas staged by the court musician, Attilio Ariosti (1660–1714). Other talented musicians, such as the famous violinist, Corelli, also performed at court, and in 1696 the eleven-year-old George Frederick Handel, a native of Halle, attracted the attention of Elector Frederick and his wife with his musical talents. Handel became the organist at the Calvinist cathedral in Halle while studying at the university, but he later moved to Hamburg and Hanover where there were better opportunities. As a young man, Johann Sebastian Bach turned down a post as organist in Halle, in favour of becoming musical director to the neighbouring Prince of Köthen. But in 1719–21, it was in fulfilment of a commission from the Great Elector's youngest son, Margrave Christian Louis, step-uncle to the reigning king, Frederick William, that Bach composed his six famous Brandenburg Concertos. In 1738, the composer's son, Carl Philipp Emmanuel Bach, was appointed court harpsichordist to the royal heir, Crown Prince Frederick, who was the first of the Hohenzollerns to have a genuine love of music.

Of all the cultural genres, the visual arts appealed most to the Great Elector and his son. This was the period of the Baroque, an ornate, vigorous and theatrical style which emanated from Rome and was celebrated in particular in the work of Gianlorenzo Bernini (1598–1680). It may seem curious that the Calvinist electors of Brandenburg should endorse a style associated so strongly with the sculpture and architecture of the Catholic Counter Reformation, but the complex expression of Baroque art in Louis XIV's Versailles had a profound effect on European taste, even in the courts of Protestant Germany.

To enhance his capital, Elector Frederick William ordered the draining and clearing of the land to the south and south-west for the development of new suburbs. Friedrichswerder was built in 1660 followed in 1678 by Dorotheenstadt, with its famous lime trees. This second suburb was named after his second wife, who had encouraged the project. An impressive fortification with bastions and ornamental gates was built to protect the city. The Great Elector also tried to stimulate the arts by inviting a number of Dutch and French artists to decorate the interior of the Electoral residences. One of these was Oranienburg, north of the capital, which Elector Frederick William gave to his Dutch first wife, Louise Henriette. In contrast to the forbidding castle (*Schloss*) in Berlin, the Great Elector built himself a country retreat at Potsdam, west of the city, which appealed to his spartan nature. Under his successors this grew into a palace. The process of enhancement began under the Elector-King Frederick, who was far less frugal and set out to glorify the state by making Berlin the cultural capital of northern Germany.

Encouraged by Danckelmann, Frederick tried to stimulate the arts by establishing a state academy in Berlin in 1696. It encompassed painting, ceramics, tapestries, jewelry, antiquities and a range of activities from design and metal-working to architecture, botanical gardening and anatomy. Renamed the Academy of Arts and Mechanical Sciences, it encouraged artists from all over Europe to visit Berlin. Meanwhile, the architect Johann Arnold Nering (1659–95) was employed to design a summer palace on the outskirts of the capital for the Electress, Sophie Charlotte, where she indulged her love of *chinoiserie* (Chinese decorative art) and enjoyed walking in the gardens which had been designed by Louis XIV's landscape architect, Le Nôtre.

After the queen's death in 1705 the Baroque building was enlarged by the king's other great architect, Andreas Schlüter (1664–1714), and renamed Charlottenburg. Schlüter had been invited to Berlin as court sculptor in 1694, and in the ensuing two decades he completed two famous Baroque masterpieces, the first a bronze statue of Frederick himself, the other the magnificent equestrian statue of the Great Elector. His decorative work was exemplified on the pulpit of the Marienkirche and the inner court of the Arsenal, while his architectural triumphs included the rebuilding of the royal palace in Berlin (destroyed in World War II) and the renovation of the old Post Office and the Arsenal. To complete the adornment of the city, Frederick had also ordered the building of a new suburb, Friedrichstadt (1688) and in 1709 the framework of a Greater Berlin was established when all the suburbs were brought together and regulated as one municipality. However, under King Frederick William the secular building programme came to a halt and Schlüter left Brandenburg for service with the Russian court. The new king had different priorities. His tastes were simple and economical, reflected in some modest church building in the Dutch classical style.

The image of the Hohenzollern state?

Unlike the grand nobility of France, Spain and the Habsburg Empire, the junker class lacked the resources to act as patrons of artists and scholars, so it fell to Brandenburg–Prussia's rulers to take the initiative in cultural matters. Like most German princes of the late seventeenth and early eighteenth centuries, the Great Elector and the Elector-King Frederick took their cue to some extent from Louis XIV of France. Frederick I, in particular, learned an important lesson from the French king, that political power was not simply a matter of economic and military strength. Monarchs needed cultural symbols such as palaces just as governments today need favourable publicity or an efficient propaganda machine. Frederick was thus prepared to invest his state's limited resources in cultural projects, but he and his son, Frederick William, were never patrons on the scale of their neighbour, Augustus the Strong of Saxony–Poland (1694–1733); as a result, Berlin could not match Dresden as a Baroque city.

The impact of France on Brandenburg–Prussia waned after 1713. From the Great Elector to King Frederick William, Calvinism was the dominant influence on the cultural philosophy of the state, and with it a belief in the puritan values of duty, thrift and hard work. The 'puritan ethic' was most evident during the reign of 'the sergeant-king'. However, conflicting tendencies were also apparent in the first half of the eighteenth century. We have already noted a disparity between 'high culture' and social progress. Another dichotomy was implicit in the contrasting styles of government of the first two Prussian kings. Frederick I, who enjoyed the benevolent role of patron to artists, Pietist scholars and refugees, favoured an environment of tolerance. His success had the effect of encouraging Rationalism, which would later help to foster the German Enlightenment. In contrast, Frederick William had little interest in artistic patronage. He reserved his admiration for qualities such as spartan self-discipline, loyalty and obedience, and the autocratic and militarist culture which he established in time came to be regarded as essentially Prussian.

Conclusion

This account cannot escape an obvious question: how do historians explain 'the rise' of a state? In the case of Sweden, attention usually focuses on its military machine and the brilliance of its soldier-kings. On the other hand, economic factors appear to be the key to the success of the Dutch Republic. But 'greatness' has more than one dimension and is also a relative value. In real terms neither seventeenth-century Brandenburg–Prussia nor Sweden nor the Dutch Republic could be seriously compared with Louis XIV's France. The population of the Hohenzollern lands was a fraction of the French populace, and the scattered territories could never sustain a comparable degree of self-sufficiency. Brandenburg–Prussia was no more than a second-class European power before 1750, and although by 1740 it had the fourth largest army in Europe, its military force – which thanks to the Great Elector and his son reached 40,000 by 1713 – could scarcely compete with Louis's Grand Army, a massive force of 360,000 men.

However, in the absence of comprehensive statistics, it is valid to look for a variety of indicators of increased status. Some evidence is subjective and impressionistic: the judgments and remarks of contemporaries recorded in letters or memoirs, architectural and engineering achievements, evidence of creativity, the association of the state with outstanding figures. The palaces of Charlottenburg and Oranienburg, for instance, or the foundation of Halle University, tell us something about Brandenburg's increased status. For in any measurable terms, there is no doubt that Brandenburg–Prussia 'rose' in the course of the seventeenth and eighteenth centuries. It expanded territorially, developed a sizeable military capacity and a large and efficient bureaucracy, and acquired considerable political prestige. This must represent a metamorphosis from the 'thinly populated, poverty-stricken sand box' of the Great Elector's reign, when the total population was between one half and three-quarters of a million, and Berlin had a mere 15,000 inhabitants.

The pace of change and improvement, however, was steady rather than spectacular. Although the population of Brandenburg–Prussia had risen to just over a million by 1700, this still made it one of the sparsely populated parts of Europe, with a population density less than one third of France, the United Provinces or Saxony. At the accession of Elector Frederick III (1688), Vienna, with a population of 80,000 inhabitants, far surpassed Berlin with its 21,500, though the latter city grew rapidly to about 60,000 by 1710. The total population of the Hohenzollern possessions increased to a modest 2–2.5 million by 1740. Only by the absorption of sizeable areas of land through diplomacy or military conquest would the population of Brandenburg–Prussia be substantially increased in the later eighteenth century.

This last point underlines one of the prime reasons for the 'rise' of Brandenburg–Prussia. Successive Hohenzollern rulers placed a high premium on territorial expansion and were prepared to go to war in the hope of making gains at the ensuing peace negotiations. Sometimes they succeeded, as when Elector Frederick William won East Pomerania, with Halberstadt, Minden, Kammin and Magdeburg; sometimes they failed, as he also discovered twice in his pursuit of West Pomerania. But the Elector–Kings saw war as a means of enforcing dynastic claims against competing powers, and Pomerania, for example, would never have been incorporated into Brandenburg–Prussia without their being prepared to resort to military conquest. The prizes of Prussian sovereignty and the royal title were also achieved after displays of armed force.

If war was one instrument of success, the dynastic treaty was another. The gradual accumulation of territory by Brandenburg–Prussia came about as the result of a number of fortuitous marriage alliances and dynastic agreements. These were the basis of their claims to ducal Prussia, Jülich-Cleves, Pomerania, parts of Silesia, East Friesland and the lands of the House of Orange. By comparison with other princely families, the Hohenzollerns were remarkably blessed by long life, virility and a lack of serious inherited disorders. Despite a tendency for ruler and heir to quarrel – evidence of a seventeenth-century generation gap – eldest sons of the line followed their fathers to the throne without any of the bitter inter-generational conflict or problems which affected other countries. As a result, Brandenburg–Prussia avoided attempted coups, disputed successions, ruling minors or unstable regencies. There was no 'War of the Prussian Succession', as there were wars to settle the succession in Russia, Sweden, England, Spain, Poland, Austria, and later in the eighteenth century, Bavaria. On the contrary, as luck would have it, Elector George William reigned virtually unchallenged for almost twenty-one years, the Great Elector for forty-eight years, King Frederick I for twenty-five years, King Frederick William I for twenty-seven years. This was a quite remarkable record of stability and continuity without which Brandenburg–Prussia may well have remained an unpretentious north German state. Historians seem to be questioning long-held judgements on the relative merit of these rulers. Yet the fact remains that good fortune, together with a sense of dynasticism, duty, and divine beneficence, enabled successive Hohenzollerns to work at the process of state-building and, by stamping their influence upon their various territories, to achieve a considerable degree of success.

Select bibliography

The following is a selection of the books which proved useful to the author.

1 Carsten, F.L., *Princes and Parliaments in Germany from the Fifteenth to the Eighteenth Century* (Oxford, 1959)
2 Carsten, F.L., *The Origins of Prussia* (4th edn, Oxford, 1968)
3 Carsten, F.L., *A History of the Prussian Junkers* (Aldershot, 1989)
4 Dorwat, R.A., *The Prussian Welfare State before 1740* (Cambridge, Mass., 1971)
5 Feuchtwanger, E.J., *Prussia: Myth and Reality* (London, 1970)
6 Koch, H.W., *A History of Prussia* (London, 1978)
7 Rosenberg, Hans, *Bureaucracy, Aristocracy and Autocracy: The Prussian Experience 1660–1815* (Boston, Beacon Paperback, 1966)

Certain general histories of modern Germany include sections on Brandenburg–Prussia.

8 Barraclough, G., *The Origins of Modern Germany* (Oxford, 1949, revised edn 1988)
9 Fulbrook, M., *Piety and Politics. Religion and the Rise of Absolutism in England, Wurttemberg and Prussia* (Cambridge 1983)

10 Holborn, Hajo, *A History of Modern Germany*. Vol. 1, *The Reformation*; vol.2, *1648–1840* (London, 1965)
11 Hughes, Michael, *Early Modern Germany 1477–1806*, European Studies Series (London, 1992) – sheds light in a refreshing way on many established assumptions
12 Vierhaus, Rudolph, *Germany in the Age of Absolutism*, trans. by Jonathan B. Knudsen (Cambridge, 1989)

The Thirty Years War is a controversial topic which has been the subject of both powerful propaganda and considerable modern revisionism. C.V. Wedgwood's detailed history is still the starting point for this subject, but her traditional interpretation has been much modified in a number of articles and books.

13 Lee, Stephen J., *The Thirty Years War* (Lancaster Pamphlets, 1991) – a useful, recent synthesis

14 Parker, Geoffrey, *The Thirty Years War* (London, 1984)
15 Steinberg, S.H., *The Thirty Years War and the Conflict for European Hegemony* (London, 1971)
16 Wedgwood, C.V., *The Thirty Years War* (London, 1938)

Of the many general histories of Europe it is only possible to mention a few.

17 Anderson, M.S., *War and Society in Europe of the Old Regime, 1618–1789* (Fontana Paperbacks, 1988) – discusses Prussian militarism
18 Black, Jeremy, *The Rise of the European Powers 1679–1793* (London, 1990)
19 Black, Jeremy, *Eighteenth century Europe 1700–1789* (Macmillan History of Europe, London, 1990)
20 Black, Jeremy, *A Military Revolution? Military Change and European Society 1550–1800* (Studies in European History, London, 1991)
21 Henshall, Nicholas, *The Myth of Absolutism: Change and Continuity in Early Modern European Monarchy* (London and New York, 1992) – makes some fresh observations on Brandenburg
22 Kirby, David, *Northern Europe in the Early Modern Period: The Baltic World 1492–1772* (London and New York, 1990)
23 Macartney, C.A. (ed.) *The Habsurg and Hohenzollern Dynasties in the Seventeenth and Eighteenth Centuries* (New

York, 1970) – provides translated documents and an introductory commentary reflecting the traditional interpretation of the Hohenzollerns

24 Munck, Thomas, *Seventeenth Century Europe: State, Conflict and the Social Order in Europe 1598–1700* (Macmillan History of Europe, London 1990)

There is much need for a new biography of the Great Elector, Frederick William I, to replace the outdated work of Ferdinand Schevill. The Elector-King Frederick I has been rehabilitated by Linda and Marsha Frey, but his son, King Frederick William I awaits a new study.

25 Dorwart, F.A., *The Administrative Reforms of Frederick William I of Prussia* (Cambridge, Mass., 1953)

26 Frey, L. and Frey, M., *Frederick I: The Man and His Times* (East European Monographs, Boulder & New York, 1984) – this is an informative and forthright work, valuable because it sets Frederick's reign in the context of his relationship with his father, the Great Elector, and his son, King Frederick William I

27 Schevill, F. *The Great Elector* (Chicago, 1947, 2nd edn Hamden, Conn., 1965)